I0463403

Contents

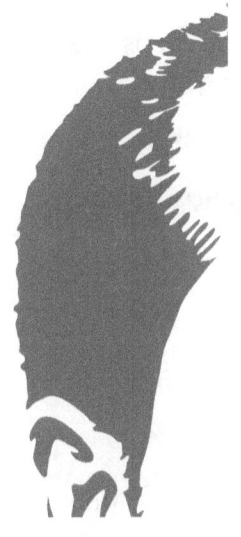

ATTRIBUTIONS

ATTRIBUTIONS

This book is dedicated to the public domain and licensed under the terms of the CC0 license.

Book Publishing: Clément Renaud

Cover Painting: Omar Ibrahim, artist born in the south of Syria 1978, living and working in Paris.

Book Production and Cover Design: Julien Taquet

Book Sprint Facilitation: Barbara Rühling

Text Clean-Up: Raewyn Whyte

MISSINGBASSEL Illustration: Neil Stuber

CONTRIBUTORS

Christopher Adams is 35 years old. He is a photographer, and published FREESOULS by JOI ITO. Christopher is a member of Fabricatorz and helps run the #FREEBASSEL campaign. He lives in Taipei.

Sabrina Banes (@missbananabiker) writes about information security, web freedoms, strong cryptography, anarcho-communism.

By The Big Conversation Space (Niki Korth & Clémence de Montgolfier) is an art and research collaborative dedicated to conversations of all shapes, sizes, and (file) formats.

Tim Boykett is involved in researches in the field of near-rings, relations between theoretical computer science and abstract algebra.

Lorna Campbell work for the University of Edinburgh. She is specialized in open education technology, policy, and practice.

Giorgos Cheliotis lives and works in Athens. He is a close observer of networks, internet cultures, sociotechnical and policy issues in new media.

Tyng-Ruey Chuang led Creative Commons Taiwan. His research areas include functional programming, programming languages and systems, XML and Web technologies, and social implications of information technologies.

ginger coons is a digital researcher, a f-loss design advocate, and editor of @libgraphicsmag.

Ben Dablo is a 31 year old citizen wanderer living in Portland, Oregon.

Georges Dahdouh is a 37 years old Syrian designer and 3D artist. He is located in Dubai.

Patrick W. Deegan is a researcher, focus on new media art practice, sociology, and ethics. He is also a freelance curator and developer at Fabricatorz.

Dr. Martin Paul Eve is a senior lecturer in literature, technology and publishing. He lives in London.

Pauline Gadea is 30 years old. She lives in Toulouse. After years in the media, Pauline now works in local food craft products.

Lucas Gonze is a product innovator, hacker, creative technologist.

Richard Goodman is the E-Learning Systems Team Manager in IT Services at Loughborough University.

Shauna Gordon-McKeon is a U.S. writer, independent researcher and developer. She focuses on open technologies and communities.

Christian Grothoff is maintainer of GNU Taler.

A global nomad, hellekin is a free software activist, member of the Dyne.org Foundation, and GNU consensus maintainer.

Adam Hyde is the founder of BookSprints.

Pete Ippel's art is conceptual in nature and spans a variety of media from the traditional to the cutting edge. Pete's personal account is @hypermodern.

Jaromil is a member of the Dyne.org Foundation and the D-CENT project.

Muid Latif is a Malaysian-based web designer, graphic designer and digital artist.

Lawrence Lessig is an American academic, and political activist. He is the founder of Creative Commons and Rootstrikers.

Yu Li is 31 years old. She lives and works between Geneva and Shenzhen. Yu is a researcher, interaction and speculative designer.

Mike Linksvayer is a dilettante of various free knowledge movements and a sub-dilettante critic of the same.

Geert Lovink is a Dutch-Australian media theorist and critic. He is the founding director of the Institute of Network Cultures, Amsterdam.

Sulaïman Majali is an artist based in Glasgow, Scotland. His works question the relationships between the sculptural object and the photographic image in the mythologies of our imagined communities.

Jean Noël Montagné, founder of a hackerspace in Nice,

France, called Nicelab, "Open Laboratory of Nice".

Jon Phillips is the co-founder of design and technology company Fabricatorz. He lives in Hong Kong. Jon founded the #FREEBASSEL campaign in 2012. Transcript by Ekta Saran.

Théophile Pillault is 33 years old. He lives in Marseille. Théophile is a freelance journalist, working for Vice, Les Inrockuptibles or Trax Magazine.

radium is a member of the Dyne.org Foundation and the D-CENT project.

Donatella Della Ratta has been managing the Creative Commons Arab world community for five years. She maintains a blog on Arab media at `http://mediaoriente.com` and tweets avidly @donatelladr.

Clément Renaud is a 32-years old researcher, developer, creative coder, and journalist based in Lyon.

Faraj Rifait is Bassel's uncle.

Mélanie Dulong de Rosnay is a researcher at french institution CNRS Institute for Communication Sciences where she is in charge of the Information and Commons Governance research group.

Natacha Roussel is a f-loss artist. She is the co-founder of the F-lat collective. Natacha is based in Brussels.

Noura Ghazi Safadi is a Syrian writer. She's married to Bassel.

Anasuya Sengupta is an advocate, strategist, and storyteller, currently on the Board of Directors of the Nonprofit Quarterly, an online and print publication that promotes an active and engaged democracy. She previously headed the Grantmaking department at the Wikimedia Foundation, and the Asia Pacific portfolio at the Global Fund for

Women.

Designer, technologist, and apparently author, Barry Threw (@barrythrew) is the Director of Software at Obscura Digital, curator with Gray Area Foundation for the Arts, and the Interim Director of the #NEWPALMYRA project. He lives in San Francisco, CA.

Stéphanie Vidal is 30 years old. She is a cultural journalist specialised in new media and digital strategist. Stéphanie lives in Paris.

Marc Weidenbaum publishes a webzine, Disquiet, about electronic ambient music and has contributed to the scientific journal Nature upon this subject. He was editor-in-chief for two of Viz Media's magazines. He lives in San Francisco.

John Wilbanks is the Chief Commons Officer at Sage Bionetworks and a Senior Fellow at the Ewing Marion Kauffman Foundation and at FasterCures. He ran the Science Commons project at Creative Commons.

Maarten Zeinstra is an advisor copyright law and technology in the cultural sector for Nederlands agency Kennisland. He lives in Amsterdam.

Mushon Zer-Aviv is a designer, an educator and a media activist. He is based in Tel Aviv.

Ethan Zuckerman, Director, Center for Civic Media, MIT Media Lab, where Bassel was offered a researcher position on October 22, 2015.

ANNOUNCEMENT

Dear reader, this book has been a huge effort by many people from around the world. The sole focus of our efforts is to bring to the attention of you, the reader, the following link: http://freebassel.org We would be very happy if you were to honor our efforts by visiting that link and adding your name to the campaign to Free Bassel.

#costoffreedom

#freebassel

PROLOGUE

VOICES OF FREE CULTURE

Clément Renaud

This book was written in Pourrières, France, in five days, from 2nd to 6th November 2015.

Just two weeks before, I got a phone call from a friend, asking me to help bring attention to the plight of Bassel Khartabil, by organizing this book. We jumped into the project instantly, starting to pull people together, authoring web pages and open calls, sending emails and calling everyone we could think of.

The book you are reading is the result of this emergent process, based on friendship, internal networks, and external publications.

It originates with our friend Bassel, suffering in a Syrian jail that has taken him away from us. I have never met him, but I am calling him a friend because I know from all who have known him that I will have a good time meeting, talking, and working with him.

In the small group of "free culture" we tend to regard each other as friends. We all feel committed to a common mission. For this book, we made an open call to those who have "been fighting in the trenches" of free culture. That sounds like an overstatement for most of us who are not in jail but are instead mostly writing, coding and taking part in interesting projects, enjoying our freedom.

Thus, when we call for a reflection on "the Cost of Freedom", we suddenly appeal not to our group and our mission, but to each individual that has been part of it. Instead of preaching the values of a whole system supposedly based on commons and sharing, we target people in their daily lives – those who have suffered from loneliness, questioning,

3

bankruptcy, burnout, exploitation, and even from seeing friends and partners suddenly missing, just for having been a part of free culture.

This book is not a statement about freedom and culture; it is a primal scream, the sum of our questions and desires. It is the raw expression of our lives. It talks about what is ultimately made through the dream of free culture: us.

This book is dedicated to Bassel Khartabil and to all those that will recognize themselves in the stories told in these pages.

INTRODUCTION

Freedom comes with many costs, not least responsibility. Social, psychological, financial, bodily, emotional: known and unknown costs, often to bystanders, make any strategy to gain and protect freedom an ambiguous quest. Sometimes it isn't clear what freedom means. Many people use and produce bits of free knowledge, but any serious attempt quickly runs into tremendous barriers, in every field. Participants receive unequal welcome due to gender, language, cultural or economic differences. Occasionally, the production of intangible assets may intersect with broader historical movements, redefining their meanings and exposing their participants to unlimited costs.

Considering the costs borne by millions to obtain, for example, freedom from slavery or freedom to vote, free knowledge movements seem rather safe and straightforward. By contrast, to consider the costs of free culture, free software or open scientific research may look adventurous, or perhaps just presumptuous. But this is what we will attempt to do, with appropriate humility. This book wants to discuss how free knowledge movements are built and the real costs attached to them. Activists, artists, designers, developers, researchers, and writers involved with free knowledge movements have worked together to see further than the fog of our news feeds and produce some sense from our different experiences.

This book is born in an attempt to free Bassel Khartabil, loved and celebrated Internet volunteer detained in Syria since 15 March 2012. His name has been deleted from the Adra Prison's register where he was detained, on 3 October 2015. We have not received any information about his current status or whereabouts since. The introductory part of this book called Collective Memory gives voice to his friends and family that have been urging for his release and want him back in his normal life and freedom, immediately.

Seeing Bassel paying a high price for his participation in free culture, many of us have started to reflect on our own fates, actions, and choices. Why are we here today? What have we chosen? What have we given up in this process of sometimes extreme belief? The second part, OPENING: FREEDOM, is a recollection of personal, sometimes contradictory reflections and views about the experience of working within free culture for some years. The diversity of contributions express the many directions that have been taken to act.

The third part called ARCHITECTONICS OF POWER takes a step back to look at how we, as a society, deal or fail to deal with the different barriers that stand in our ways towards freedom. Different authors analyze the contradictions of their choices and daily activities with larger objectives and lifestyles associated with free culture. The variety of professions and situations of the contributors offer an illustration stained with multiple tones.

Finally, the fourth part AFFORDANCES offers a reflection on theories and successful practices of free culture. It offers different perspectives on the nature, structure, motivations and limitations of existing levers towards liberation, not only legal and technological but also social and cultural.

Once marginal, free culture is today on the edge of becoming part of the new normal thanks to the Internet while being threatened in its fundamentals by its own success. The many contributions in this book offer a unique snapshot of its dreads and interrogations, and a tentative program for the reader to reflect on the future of freedom in our times.

COLLECTIVE
MEMORY

THE UNCOMMON CREATIVITY OF BASSEL KHARTABIL

Barry Threw

The people who are in real danger never leave their countries. They are in danger for a reason and for that they don't leave #Syria

@basselsafadi on Twitter, 1/31/2012 14:34:46, one month before detention.

In October 2010, I sat at a checkpoint on the Lebanon-Syria border, waiting for Bassel. It was late, and I'd been sitting in a nearby café, smelling of bleach but otherwise unremarkable, for nearly 12 hours. I was waiting with one of my traveling companions, Christopher Adams, who had been denied entry as a result of visa issues ("everything fine, stamps just changed yesterday"). We were part of a group of Creative Commons advocates traveling to Damascus as the last stop on a tour around the Arab world, doing workshops on free culture and open source software, along with such community stalwarts as Joi Ito, Lawrence Lessig, Mitchell Baker, Jon Phillips, and Bassel himself. It was a group from the near-future, time traveling at a second-per-second to the oldest still-inhabited city in existence, a place outside of time.

It was clear, after much whispered negotiation between Bassel and the border police, that Christopher wouldn't be admitted via one of the usual persuasions employed to skirt the bureaucratic impasses typical for that part of the world. Bassel spent several hours on his cell phone, serially calling government offices of murky authority, but eventually it became apparent that a resolution required in-person meetings. Bassel and the majority of our crew left for Damascus, leaving Chris and me to enjoy the landscape, a sepia liminal space of Martian desert and cinder-block buildings where used washing machines and cell phones were sold. As the night wore on and nothing changed Chris went back to Beirut, and I sat while Bassel allegedly made his way back for me.

These moments didn't stand out to me at the time, but it was here I first was affected with great admiration and respect for Bassel Khartabil, through watching his tireless commitment to his friends, and later learning of his larger efforts enabling access to knowledge, preserving cultural heritage, and fostering free creative expression. The projects he's created and supported, the artifacts left behind, reveal an astonishing intuition for issues holding back society in Syria and globally, and a singular vision for building technical and social ways to address them. Organizing this trip to Damascus for luminaries of the open culture/free software movement was exemplary of what brings him joy: bringing his friends and colleagues together, and sharing the knowledge and experience of his home.

Bassel Khartabil was born in Syria in 1981 of a Palestinian father and Syrian mother. Although born in a culture known for its conservatism and adherence to tradition, he was raised as the only child in a liberal and creative household; his father, Jamil, a writer, and his mother, Raya, a piano professor. As with many only-children, Bassel was most at home inside his own curiosity and creativity. An avid reader, he devoured advanced books on the ancient history of the Middle East, and Greek mythology, from a young age. He was also a natural self-learner and taught himself English from a CD-ROM on his father's computer. He was drawn to computers, helping his father research online, and learning to program in C. This fascination and facility with technology continued throughout his upbringing, fixing his family computers, learning advanced programming for desktop and the web, and joining the communities dedicated to advancing and upholding the openness and creativity that he cherished. He was raised in a place of rich history and tradition, but lives in a global world of technology; a man outside of time.

Bassel, like many of us, found Freedom within technology, and tried to share that freedom with others, but he did not yet know the cost.

If there is one thing always said about Bassel by the people that know him best, it is that he loves to share is knowledge with anyone who asks. For two weeks we lived out of AikiLab, the "hackerspace" he founded in Damascus, giving workshops and lectures, and meeting the young community that came to listen. The space was for more than just events, it was a social gathering place, where knowledge was shared, and new friends and collaborations made. Inside were computers, projectors, the Internet, all of the equipment needed to provide education and support to the nascent Syrian tech culture. But, the vital element was not the gear or even AikiLab, but Bassel himself. Even when he was confined in Adra prison, Bassel found time to teach the other prisoners English and about technology, even though they had no computers available.

But, even more than education, Bassel's true gift is Protoculture, developing the near-future alpha versions of projects catalyzing change in cultural contexts, whether software tools, community organization, or digital art. His Aiki web development framework allowed multiple developers to work simultaneously on a live web site, while maintaining security. It was used to build still active open content projects such as the Open Clip Art Library and Open Font Library. His platforms, whether physical, social, or digital enable new projects to spring up, and the community to build on its self.

Perhaps none of Bassel's cultural prototypes were more

prescient than the work he started around 2005, with a group of archeologists and 3D artists, to virtually reconstruct the ancient ruins of Palmyra. One of the world's most important archaeological sites, Palmyra stood at the crossroads of several civilizations, with Graeco-Roman architectural styles melding with local traditions and Persian influences. Little could Bassel know that ten years after he began, Daesh fundamentalists would be actively deleting this architecture embodying Syrian, and the world's, cultural heritage. But his foray into digital archaeology and preservation created a time capsule that will be invaluable to the public, researchers, and artists for years to come.

Tragically, Bassel has not yet been able to complete this project. On 15 March 2012, Bassel was imprisoned by the Assad government in a wave of arrests triggered by the civic unrest pushing for democratic freedom in Syria. The United Nations Working Group on Arbitrary Detention has determined that Bassel's arrest and imprisonment were arbitrary and in violation of international law, and has called for his immediate release. For three years, he was held in the infamous Adra prison with 7,000 others, until October 2015, when he was moved to an unknown location. As of this writing, no information has been released by the Assad government on his location or condition. The #freebassel campaign continues to fight to keep Bassel's plight in the public eye, and, ultimately, achieve his release. For Bassel, the Cost of Freedom has not been trivial or abstract, but has caused him to be separated from his community and loved ones.

We have recently launched a project building on Bassel's original work called #NEWPALMYRA. It is an online community platform and data repository dedicated to the capture, preservation, sharing, and creative reuse of data about the ancient city of Palmyra. Released under a Creative Commons CC0 license, all models and data collected are available in the public domain to remix and distribute. The project will continue, continued by its international affiliates and advisors, until Bassel's release, when he can accept his research position at the MIT Media Lab and carry it forward once again.

The #NEWPALMYRA project starts from Bassel's original vision, but goes further, creating a new community around the virtual Palmyra through open calls for participation, real world development events, and pop-up art shows. A city is built in architecture, but lived in by people, and our virtual New Palmyra will serve as a nexus for creative explorations and cultural understanding. The book you are reading is one of these related projects, bringing together writings from a diverse and insightful group of authors committed to the promise of free culture. Here we create our own time capsule, a record of thoughts on freedom and responsibility from many different perspectives and disciplines, so the next generation of digital archaeologists can learn about us.

Eventually, Bassel came walking through the dark to that checkpoint, and with more whispers to lackluster guards I was on my way to Damascus. Christopher met our group the next day, and together we all embraced Bassel's world, one of standing up for freedom, and constantly giving to his friends and community, that to this day inspires us to push further. This Uncommon Creativity, an ability to innovate and invent in the future while building on the past, is what makes him a vital visionary for the Syrian community. But, I find myself once again waiting for Bassel, this time to regain his Freedom for which he has paid so dearly.

I hope, my friend, to see you soon.

BASSEL, AND MY FREEDOM

Noura Safadi

To get married: that means your man will push you forward or take you backward.

What happened to me is that my husband has been pushing me forward in the best path possible. He makes me go upwards, fly, swim over the clouds, even though the time we've spent in love has been spent apart. He is present in all my details... and helped create who I am. I am his pen and colors, and he has always been my life and my Freedom. I've lived all my life dreaming of Freedom, and Bassel taught me to embrace it.

I feel overwhelmed when I mention his name. Bassel taught me to master English, even while he's been in prison. I've learned to read, write, and speak English well. He has always shared his knowledge with everyone who asked, and has also taught many prisoners to read, write, and speak English.

Bassel opened the door to technology for me, he taught me to use both computers and smartphones. He taught me the Internet. He also taught other prisoners to use computers theoretically, without having one in their hands.

I never felt our relationship stopped me from being myself: on the contrary he taught me to break the fear and shame of social restrictions. I've been a writer for the last 10 years, but only Bassel made me decide to write my first book. I wrote it during his lengthy detention, and we called it "In the Waiting."

With Bassel, I make my dreams come true, I learn to express my thoughts and feelings, and face my fears... I shout, I resist, I trance... I laugh and I cry...

Bassel made me Free, while he is absent. He is in the regime's jail, and I am in the jail of waiting for him.

ABOUT BASSEL

Patrick W. Deegan

Bassel Khartabil (Arabic: خرطبيل باسل) also known as Bassel Safadi (Arabic: صفدي باسل) is a software developer and community builder, an advocate for internet freedom, and most recently, and perhaps most personally, a supporter of free-access and liberty in Syria.

Bassel's work in Syria joined his numerous other international projects together into a unified and focused opus. These earlier works included worldwide work with Mozilla Firefox, Wikipedia, Openclipart, Fabricatorz, and Sharism, as well as being an initiator and key member of the Creative Commons Syria release. Khartabil also developed the novel web framework known as Aiki as a part of his own collaborative research company Aiki Lab. For its own part, Aiki codified many aspects of Bassel's own personality: surprisingly user-friendly while being technically sophisticated, Aiki is a web developer's concept of poetic code in its powerful simplicity.

Taken together, his most recent work — New Palmyra — sought to capture in a similar spirit of public openness one of the hallmarks of human civilization. New Palmyra presents a digital archive in rendered 3D of the ancient site of Palmyra. At almost every level, from process to function, and from code to metaphor, this project is as an almost perfect stand-in for Bassel himself. And perhaps it also summarizes in form and idea the fact that Bassel is presently not here.

Since mid-march of 2012 Bassel has been a prisoner of the Assad regime in Syria. No longer a country satisfied with the politics of As-If, Bassel was long an active part of asking for the very best of Syrians, for themselves and for the world. And for this, like so many of his fellow countrymen and women, he was imprisoned. But Bassel knows that a community is a powerful thing — it retains and rebuilds, it preserves and presses forward, and above all it never forgets its own.

#NEWPALMYRA AND THE FREE BASSEL CAMPAIGN

Jon Phillips

Edited by Patrick Deegan.

Bassel has been imprisoned for nearly four years, I believe it is about 1400 days now, but I have lost count; and since then we have been running the Free Bassel campaign. The most depressing thing is that he has been missing for over a month now. He was taken from the prison, and his name was removed from the list of prisoners. We really really don't know where he is. He may even have been kidnapped though it's more likely that the Assad regime has him in a military prison. So that led to an acceleration in our efforts.

One project Bassel had started before he became a political prisoner was the #NEWPALMYRA project. There are actually several projects and ideas he created that have not yet been announced, so this is the first of the many different projects we are now undertaking to help call attention to his plight, as well as the importance of his work.

The idea behind #NEWPALMYRA was to recreate the ancient city of Palmyra in 3D virtual reality. The #NEWPALMYRA project is a new online community platform and data repository dedicated to the capture, preservation, sharing, and creative reuse of data about the ancient city of Palmyra. The main idea is to focus on model quality first, and each subsequently completed section will be released into the public domain. We will release a master plan of the city and then a 3D model of the city — we want to keep moving forward on NEWPALMYRA, the city of heroes that cannot be conquered. We will release all the data under the Creative Commons Zero license, so anyone can do anything with it. We already have contributions from different places in the world. Our hope is to partner with other organizations like Creative Commons, MIT Medialab, and the Barjeel Foundation in Dubai, who we hope will become data providers and production partners on this artistic and scientific project.

That's really the historical significance of the name PALMYRA, and we are trying to embody that essence. We haven't announced the full list of projects yet, but we'll begin by announcing artists and shows from around the world about PALMYRA. So no matter what type of symbolic destruction or act happens, and we hear about the terrible things being done, we will do longer, better things. In fact, it's even more transcendant: We BUILD culture. (They destroy culture.) We extend memory. (Others forget.) We REMEMBER. We never forget about our friend. But we're also not single-mindedly political in our efforts to build up the city again. We hope it is built in as many different forms as there are builders' hands. And to that end: we need your help as well. Palmyra.org is where to join forces with us. And if you have any particular skills or photos, please share them with us. We can use those photos to create 3D models through photogrammetry.

There are two other projects that have been initiated, all linked to NEWPALMYRA, that I want to discuss here. One happened in Paris, the second took place near Aix-en-Provence. The idea is to write a book with several creative cultural producers and software developers titled "Cost of Freedom." That's something we talked a lot about with Bassel. We have it done today. So he really initiated this idea as well, and while the book as it is now has been written with a somewhat different and more urgent focus, the core of the project remains consistent with our original vision. The tech from projects—the collaborative, multiscale, interdisciplinary, and international aspects of it, as well as the actual

18

method of production and technological content—will also go into the book. And that's a powerful thing.

Part of this current idea for Cost of Freedom also comes from doing an earlier event called ProtoCultural, which was first organized in Paris in 2015. The idea was to get people together for two days and use the time, community, and derivative data to then create and generate artwork. Among the immediate fruits of that labor was an Artshow. In another case, the artist Amad Ali created an optical installation from the columns of the Temple of Bel. In deference to that but in a more playful mood, Christopher Adams from Fabricators/Free Souls made a #NEWPALMYRA drink at the event. The press was there, and we were

getting a lot of attention and a lot of coverage. The reason was simple: because it's such an outrage to destroy our shared heritage. So now that we've done ProtoCultural Paris we plan on doing ProtoCultural Dubai. Then we're going to do ProtoCultural Beirut in a couple of weeks. And then ProtoCultural London. There are also several other cities we have yet to announce. But we've had a lot of success scaling events, and we're going to scale this to at least a hundred different cities around the world. If you live in a city or even a town or any interesting location, then let's do it. Let's do a ProtoCultural event. You share with us; we share together.

Our next step of many leads us to Dubai. Dubai is a really amazing city. For some reason, I have never really been present in Dubai. But I know a little about the city, and it's interesting to see Gulf futurism—an expression I borrow from our friend Sophia Al Maria. This is an apt expression because maybe #NEWPALMYRA will be like this, maybe we can build it up, right out of the desert. We can raise it up. We can build it in space. Or we can build it just online. Everyone's welcome in PALMYRA. There's no people without land. There's no problem there. We'll just create more land if we need it. So I think Dubai is an inspiration for us because if you can lift the buildings like bar graphs to the sky, then things can happen.

PALMYRA 3D, PREMONITION VISION OF BASSEL

Faraj Rifait

Born from a Palestinian father, writer, and Syrian mother, Professor of Piano, Bassel lived in an environment open to the world and remote from any conservatism. From his early childhood, reading was a refuge for the only child of the family. While children of his age were playing with toy cars, Bassel had already gone beyond the comic and was devouring books about the ancient history of the Middle East and Greek mythology.

Living in France, while Bassel grew up, one day he surprised me by speaking to me in English with a very rich vocabulary. He was only 10 years old. I asked him if he had learned English at his school in the Palestinian camp in Damascus. He smiled slyly and replied that it was through his father's computer, using a CD that he had learned English.

At 11, he had his own computer, donated by his mother for his birthday. I was expecting that he would play computer games, but I was wrong. Bassel showed me his computer programs in C language and translations into English and Arabic of some historical books. Thus, he helped his father in his research and writing his books on history.

I was surprised to see him acquire advanced technical skills for a 12 or 13-year-old boy, but Bassel told me that his uncle Osama, a computer expert at the time, helped him to develop his natural gifts. Two years later, Osama assured me that now it was he who asked advice from Bassel. As a teenager, Bassel appeared to me very passionate when he resolved computer programming, sometimes very complex projects. It seemed that Bassel was traveling through the computer world and the history of his country in a very special and multidimensional way.

It is from this double passion for history and computer programming that Bassel began working on technical projects like the creation of a web site on the discovery of the archaeological treasures of Syria. He was barely twenty years when he begun the Palmyra project in 3D, in close collaboration with Khaled al-Assa'ad, the great expert of Palmyra history, who was beheaded by Daech in 2015.

Bassel has a great intuition as if prescient, that may explain why he initiated this beautiful and ambitious project to safeguard the memory of this outstanding universal site. Bassel wishes that everyone could reinforce and contribute to embellish this multidimensional work in these troubled days until his release from jail...

REBUILD ASAD AL-LAT

Georges Dahdouh

Allat Lion, Palmyra, picture by Mappo

Watching the news in Syria, bloodshed and destruction everywhere, we have mixed feelings, fear for our parents and friends in the country facing all these atrocities, and there's nothing that we can do. The scene of an ISIS member destroying Asad Al-Lat statue with a hammer triggered it all, the statue of a lion protecting a deer, with an ancient script on its left leg, saying that bloodshed is prohibited.

We can fight this particular crime, a crime against humanity, because what they destroyed in Palmyra besides many other areas, is the world's heritage. They want these statues, this heritage, to disappear forever, but we will make the memory of these statues reach every corner in the world: this is how this project aims to resist destruction and ignorance.

We will provide open source 3D models of as much as we can of the Syrian statues, focusing on those that have been destroyed, so anyone worldwide can download, 3D print or use them in their applications, and eventually make an online museum to exhibit these 3D replicas. This project cannot compensate for the loss of those priceless masterpieces, but at least we can still keep them in the memories of successive generations.

SUPPORTING BASSEL

Ethan Zuckerman

Bassel Khartabil has been imprisoned in Syria since 2012 for the vague "crime" of "harming state security". Near as anyone can tell, his crime was in being an advocate for the use of the Internet as a platform for free speech. Through his promotion of open source software, his leadership of the Syrian Creative Commons community, and his work building innovative new publishing platforms, Bassel worked to connect Syria with the rest of the world, and to ensure that all Syrians – supporters of Assad and opponents - could make their voices heard online, even if they could not express themselves in physical space.

Our work on Civic Media at the MIT Media Lab stems from the idea that making media is a way of making change in the world. Bassel's work is in the best spirit of Civic Media, working to connect contemporary Syrians to global conversations while preserving Syria's rich history and culture. Before his unjust incarceration, Bassel was working to build a 3D model of the ancient city of Palmyra, much of which has been destroyed by ISIS fighters in the past few months. At this tragic moment in history, Syria is losing its physical history to religious fanatics while persecuting the people who could be building their digital future.

WHAT DOES FREEDOM MEAN TO YOU, MR. GOVERNMENT?

Anasuya Sengupta

Bassel Safadi, Tural Abbasli, Fariba Pajouh. Teesta Setalvad, Eskinder Nega, Raif Badawi. Anna Politkovskaya, Irom Sharmila, Aaron Swartz. Liu Xiaobo, Edward Snowden, Fereshteh Ghazi.[1]

So many names, so many faces, so many breaths. Choking, or gasping, or... gone. Many more names, many more faces, many more breaths - Unknown, unseen, unheard... Gone?

Do you know these names, Mr. Government? Do you feel their breath? Do you remember their faces, Mr. Government? Did you read what they said?

They asked for freedom, Mr. Government - Not for war. They ask for peace, Mr. Government, To be as we are.

Freedom is not a choice, Mr. Government - but you have made it a place. Hidden from all but the wealthiest, Open to a privileged gaze.

The breath remains, Mr. Government, As does the word - So long as freedom is a place, Mr. Government, Its echoes will be heard.

---

[1]These are names of journalists/writers/Internet activists from different parts of the world who have been harassed, imprisoned, or disappeared by their governments in the past few years. This list of names is obviously not meant to be either comprehensive, or representative; it invokes poetic license to remind us of what – and who – is at stake.

BASSEL K

Marc Weidenbaum

I read "The Trial" at too young an age. It instilled in me many things, some of them even positive, such as an affection for Franz Kafka, an aspiration to taut structure, and a desire to tell stories. It also haunted me, and it does to this day. It imprinted on me an intense fear of undeserved imprisonment.

I was introduced to the imprisonment of Bassel Khartabil by three remarkable people: Niki Korth, Jon Phillips, and Barry Threw. They are in many admirable ways as free as Bassel is not. Each of the trio is dedicated to their own individual and collective artistic pursuits to explore the deep potential where technology and culture meet. They make and celebrate the things that make today a special time.

And they know full well that all is not right in our time. They expend significant energy in building awareness of the ongoing fact of Bassel's murky, tragic legal status. At their suggestion, back in January 2014, I gathered musicians to highlight Bassel's plight. These musicians participate collectively in something called the Disquiet Junto. It's a freeform group I moderate that each Thursday responds to music-composition prompts. The idea behind all the prompts is that creative constraints, such as those employed in Oulipo and Fluxus, are a useful springboard for creativity and productivity.

The Junto's fondness for such "constraints" met a fierce complement when we tackled Bassel's situation, which is that of a most uncreative form of constraint. There were many ways we could have paid tribute to Bassel. What we elected to do in the Junto was to keep one of his projects

26

going: he may be in jail, but his art could continue to develop. Prior to Bassel's arrest on March 15, 2012, in Damascus, he was working on several projects. Among them was a three-dimensional computer rendering of the ancient city of Palmyra. What we in the Junto did was make "fake field recordings," audio of what the halls of Palmyra's structures might have sounded like millennia ago. Much as Bassel was trying to revive an ancient world, the Junto participants were, in essence, keeping one of his projects alive while he is incapable of doing so. And, of course, building upon his artistic efforts was true to the ethos of the Creative Commons, in which Bassel has been profoundly engaged.

We had no idea, of course, back in early 2014, that Palymra would itself receive worldwide attention when ISIS, the extremist movement, would in 2015 move to destroy much of the ancient city's remaining architectural history, or that, later still, Russian warplanes would further damage the site. This is one of Kafka's lasting legacies: just when things seem horrible, they can and do get worse.

Palmyra has fallen. Bassel remains in jail. The challenge to rectify his situation has long since surpassed the overly employed term "Kafkaesque." Someone must have been telling lies about Bassel K, because he is still kept from his freedom. But as long as he is in prison, there are plenty of people telling his story, and keeping his work alive.

MY FRIEND IS NOT FREE

Tyng-Ruey Chuang

Most of the time it came down to emotion. It was anger, frustration, exhaustion, feeling alone, confusion, and wanting to escape it all. You wished there would be hope. But it was hopeless. It was endless. It didn't get through. You were talking the same thing over again. You were back to face the same wall. You talked to many people: new people, different people, the same people. They didn't understand! You were looping in angst. There was no way to stop.

You were there. You have been there. You are standing here but you are still there as the emotion is here is there is everywhere.

Getting to freedom is not cost free. My friend it is not free. MY FRIEND IS NOT FREE.

很多時候這是情緒。憤怒、挫折、極度疲憊、孤單、困惑、想要逃避這一切。你期盼著希望。但全然無望。沒有止境。過不去。同樣的事情,你講了又講。再度面壁。你跟許多人講過:新見面的人、不同的人、同樣的人。他們不懂!你在焦慮中打轉。停不下來。

你曾到過那裡。你一直在那裡。你現站在這裡,但你還處於那裡,在這裡在那裡在在是情緒。

要得自由並非不需代價。我的朋友自由並非不需代價。我的朋友不得自由,付出了代價。

LIBERTÉ

Donatella Della Ratta

Sur mes cahiers d'écolier
Sur mon pupitre et les arbres
Sur le sable sur la neige
J'écris ton nom

Sur toutes les pages lues
Sur toutes les pages blanches
Pierre sang papier ou cendre
J'écris ton nom

Sur les images dorées
Sur les armes des guerriers
Sur la couronne des rois
J'écris ton nom

Sur la jungle et le désert
Sur les nids sur les genêts
Sur l'écho de mon enfance
J'écris ton nom

Sur les merveilles des nuits
Sur le pain blanc des journées
Sur les saisons fiancées
J'écris ton nom

Sur tous mes chiffons d'azur
Sur l'étang soleil moisi
Sur le lac lune vivante
J'écris ton nom

Sur les champs sur l'horizon
Sur les ailes des oiseaux
Et sur le moulin des ombres
J'écris ton nom

Sur chaque bouffée d'aurore
Sur la mer sur les bateaux
Sur la montagne démente
J'écris ton nom

Sur la mousse des nuages
Sur les sueurs de l'orage
Sur la pluie épaisse et fade
J'écris ton nom

Sur les formes scintillantes
Sur les cloches des couleurs
Sur la vérité physique
J'écris ton nom

Sur les sentiers éveillés
Sur les routes déployées
Sur les places qui débordent
J'écris ton nom

Sur la lampe qui s'allume
Sur la lampe qui s'éteint
Sur mes maisons réunies
J'écris ton nom

Sur le fruit coupé en deux
Du miroir et de ma chambre
Sur mon lit coquille vide
J'écris ton nom

Sur mon chien gourmand et tendre
Sur ses oreilles dressées
Sur sa patte maladroite
J'écris ton nom

Sur le tremplin de ma porte
Sur les objets familiers
Sur le flot du feu béni
J'écris ton nom

Sur toute chair accordée
Sur le front de mes amis
Sur chaque main qui se tend
J'écris ton nom

Sur la vitre des surprises
Sur les lèvres attentives
Bien au-dessus du silence
J'écris ton nom

Sur mes refuges détruits
Sur mes phares écroulés
Sur les murs de mon ennui
J'écris ton nom

Sur l'absence sans désir
Sur la solitude nue
Sur les marches de la mort
J'écris ton nom

Sur la santé revenue
Sur le risque disparu
Sur l'espoir sans souvenir
J'écris ton nom

Et par le pouvoir d'un mot
Je recommence ma vie
Je suis né pour te connaître
Pour te nommer

Liberté.

> – Paul Éluard, *Liberté*[2]
> in *Poésies et vérités*, 1942

Paul Eluard wrote this poem called "Liberté" in the darkest moment of the world's history, during World War II. At the time, France was occupied by Nazis. Violence, destruction, death were everywhere. The world was hopeless and with a very dark future ahead.

Yet words of hope were still alive, and poets such as Eluard were able to give shapes and sounds to these words. Freedom, Liberté.

Libertà, Hurriyya. I've never heard such a beautiful word being spoken by a human voice as much as when I heard this word resonating in the country I love the most, Syria.

It was the chant of life. It was about people telling the world, telling themselves: we are a-l-i-v-e!
You, my dear friend, have taken this word well above the cage of silence where it was exiled.
You, the Syrian youth, many of our friends who were rushing to write "freedom" on the city's walls, everywhere, are now paying the price.

It's dark time, just like when Paul wrote his ode to lib-

---

[2]Editor's note: we could not provide the English translation of the poem of Paul Eluard because it's copyrighted and the translator didn't want to participate. Therefore we provide the original French version which is in the Public Domain.

erté. It's dark time, my friend, and that's why we need you and your words more than ever.

That sweet sound, the sound of spring coming, the sound of youth..will come back..with you, my friend.
Hurriyya.

FREE BASSEL

Maarten Zeinstra and Muid Latif

OPENING:
FREEDOM

KEEPING PROMISES

Lawrence Lessig

Presentation by Lawrence Lessig, CC Global Summit 2015, 15 Oct 2015, Seoul, Korea Edited by Christopher Adams, 3 Nov 2015, Pourrières, France.

It's important for us elders to remind you kids of where you come from. The Creative Commons project was the failure of a legal action. When I was at the Harvard Law School in the late 1990s, Congress passed the Sony Bono Copyright Term Extension Act, which extended the term of existing copyrights by 20 years. We brought a lawsuit on behalf of a man named Eric Eldred, an online publisher who wanted to publish the poems of Robert Frost, which were to pass into the public domain, and would have passed into the public domain, had Congress not extended for the eleventh time in 40 years the existing terms of copyright.

As a law professor, as someone who had no desire to be an activist, I learned of Eric Eldred and reached out to him to say, "Why don't we challenge this decision by Congress, because it seems so plainly inconsistent with the idea of copyright for a limited time?"

We brought his case all the way to the Supreme Court, but just before we got there, Eric Eldred said to me, "Look, I appreciate what you're doing, but I don't think we're going to win, and I don't want this just to be a lawsuit, so I want you to promise me you will start a foundation committed to the Commons."

I was convinced we were going to win, so I thought, "Okay, I can make that promise, because if I win I don't have to start the foundation." I made the promise, but then I lost the case in the Supreme Court. That defeat gave birth to you, because once we lost, I had to deliver on the promise that I'd made to Eric Eldred, and so a number of us sat down in some offices in Harvard, and figured out how we would build what would become the Creative Commons.

The proudest moment I remember from those early days was the way we brought a young technical community into what seemed to be just a legal argument. One of the early victories for me was persuading a young boy of 14 or 15 years of age, named Aaron Swartz, to become the technical architect of the Creative Commons, in 2002. It took a little persuading, but I told him that this is what he had to do.

Later the relationship of me telling Aaron what he had to do reversed itself. In 2007, I was finishing my last book on copyright and Internet policy. Aaron came to visit and asked me what I was working on.

I was very proud to show him my book, and tell him about my first TED talk. Then he asked, "Why do you think you're going to make any progress on copyright and Internet policy so long as we live with a deeply corrupted government?" I told him, "It's not my field, it's not what I do." He asked, "You mean as an academic?" I said, "Yes, as an academic. It's not my field. I am a scholar of copyright, and the Internet." Aaron said, "Ok, but what about as a citizen?"

What he did at that moment was to shame me into leaving this movement, a movement that he had joined when I shamed him into building the architecture of Creative Commons. He shamed me into leaving that movement to take up a fight which has grown and has consumed my life, and consumed my life right at the moment when many of us feel we failed him, when he felt the burden of fights that he was in, in such a profound way that he had to take his own life.

That transformation led me away. But there's nothing that gives me joy like looking back at things that I had something to do with starting, and seeing them flourish, and to see the spread of ideas which the Creative Commons community has carried forward.

THE SHIT OF FREEDOM

Giorgos Cheliotis

Somebody once told me that freedom is one of these words you can't define without it becoming self-referential. A person will usually start a sentence with "freedom is when you're free to..." and their minds will hesitate for a moment: a brief, unsettling glimpse at the turtles that spiral all the way down. Few can stare into the abyss for long, so they will quickly stumble back to the comfort of the known and pick their favorite from a laundry list of personal wishes, desires, and learned ideals, except perhaps if that person is an academic, trained in words and systems of thought. There's probably many valiant attempts at a definition out there, and I'm sure that on this very day a Ph.D. student somewhere is doing a literature review on freedom and is insanely bored with it.

It is like that with universal, deeply rooted, almost primal human desires. It is like that with freedom. We think we know it when we feel it, we sometimes know it when we see it in others, but the words are hard to come by. We struggle to produce a concise definition; we struggle with the very concept of it, and at some point in our lives we wonder how free we really are, and what freedoms are perhaps worth fighting for. This, then, is the greater cost of freedom: its pursuit. I guess what I'm saying, and I know this won't please the reader, is that our natural state of being, for most if not all of human history, has been NOT free. It starts with family; then our boss; the state; the market; even our partners and friends.

Yet, for all that socialization entails, for all the grooming into conformity and compliance, for all the rules that we impose on ourselves and others, we will rebel many times over. And every time there will be a price to pay. Some will pay the ultimate price. My friend Bassel, for example, he pursued freedom of information in a land that couldn't face itself, let alone a free spirit that soared above its arid lands. Like Aaron Swartz, who pursued freedom of information in a market that trades in commodities and not ideals; like Chelsea Manning, who pursued freedom of information in a land that associates freedom with weapons, war, and the power to abduct and incarcerate. Like the founders of Pirate Bay, whose names I cannot recount, but whose services I have often used for my teaching, research, and entertainment; and like countless others, who will never make headlines. It is a sign of our times, that some of us seek freedom in information, and that some will pay an inordinately high price for it. Our age is the information age. And we are not as free as we think.

I could leave it at that. I meant to write a brief commentary on the cost of freedom. It's nothing special, but it's kind of neatly wrapped up there. However, I felt the need to say something more, something more personal and probably more important. To say it out loud, and ruffle some feathers: first my own, as I'm getting out of my comfort zone here, then those of some prancing peacocks in the free culture / FLOSS / digital rights scene, and the technopreneurs peddling freedom for dollars and fame. You see, dear reader, there are other, hidden costs to the whole endeavour of digital liberation... they're everywhere, inside and outside, in movements and in people, such as disillusionment, waste, the cost of stupidity, as a friend put it. I warn you now, this will get ugly. It needs to be. If you know me, you'll know I'm rather measured in my words and actions, even if not docile. But here I won't be. You'll be offended. In fact, I hope you will be. As much as I also seek the validation of others, I will now pay the cost of expressing myself freely. With little inhibition.

And that is because, in many of my efforts to engage

40

productively with the project of digital liberation and assorted anxieties of our time, there you were, my friend. The free software programmer that grossly overstates their contribution; the free culture evangelist who's in it for personal gain and will happily privilege their culture over everybody else's; the opportunist entrepreneur and peddler of freedom through code. You have spent a fair share of your life building things. Building tools, networks and communities. Instigating projects and influencing people, converting them to your cause, forging friendships and partnerships; gathering resources to build the world you desire. You are well educated, and you understand networks. In short, you have super powers. You have gained the respect of many and probably made some enemies along the way. You have a posse, your own personal echo chamber. You come to events and gatherings filled with the contagious energy that we all love you for. You speak of awesomeness, projects, personal freedom, a friend in peril perhaps, a worthy cause for all to rally around, a call from the White House, a famous dissident, a Nobel Laureate, a Saudi prince. Networks of power, culture and code. You gather resources. You make phone calls. You entertain and motivate. You sound important. There is something about you. In your presence, names drop like flies and jokes fly like bullets. You're awesome. And you're so full of shit.

You're always on the go. You forget things, you complicate things, you exhaust yourself and others. You rarely forget to pack your ego, though. Sometimes you manage to squeeze it all into your suitcase, with a toothbrush, t-shirts, and chargers for your beloved gadgets. But your ego is so large and overbearing, you couldn't possibly fit it in your luggage at all times. So you wear it on your sleeve. You armour yourself with layer upon layer of ego steel. You prance about, crack a joke, or two... or three... because you're awesome. You make a nice gesture, make a plan, and seek the admiration of those around you more than anything else. You make more promises than you'll ever be able to keep. You make more plans than you will ever follow up on. You make things fun. You make people believe in themselves. You make them believe your shit. I think you believe it too. I'm happy to know you. But you're so full of shit.

So is your posse, that echo chamber you've built for yourself which reinforces the best and the worst in you. Together you peddle freedom to make money, to peddle more freedom, to make more money. Sound familiar? Yeah, it's what the US government does to the world.

What are the means and what is the end in what you do? I doubt you know the answer. I only observe the briefest moments of reflection from you and your buddies on what it is we're doing here. Faint rays of meaning in a cloud of technobabble, freedombabble and babble babble.

You know I love you. You know I want to. I am charmed by your presence, laugh at your jokes, and I have made some vaguely awesome plans with you in the past. I too am a rather privileged white male who enjoys the globetrotting lifestyle, the random jokes, the occasional debauchery, the endless speculation over the next big thing, the code that binds us all into one super-network of super-friends. But knowing you a little too well, and being less gullible than I once was, I can see right through your bullshit. And there's so much of it. Sometimes I know you're trolling. Sometimes I wish you were. Sometimes I think you're just trolling yourself.

I have made mistakes in the past. I have missed deadlines. I have failed to meet goals. I have disappointed others. But I am trying to make peace with that. I try to speak less and listen more, focus on what's important, to be strong without being an ass, to be there for others, as much as I also need others to be there for me. To respect others, give them room to breathe, follow their lead when they know best, lead them when they ask me to, work with them, not have them work for me under false pretenses. Still, I fail often. Too often. I am aware of that. Are you? And what do you do about it?

I'm not ashamed of my failings, not too much at least. Nor should you be. I know you sometimes are. Is this why you never stop? Is this why you're always on the move and never ever shut up? Is this why you hate stillness? Self-reflection is a downer, right? So is contemplating the cost of freedom and the vapidness of so many of your projects. I know the drill: invest in a huge number of things, because only one or two in a thousand will succeed and make you somebody you so desire to be. Of course, this only works if you can keep the cost ridiculously low and make sure you contribute next to nothing to any single project yourself. It's all about long tails and downside risks and cheap labor. I've read the blogs and talked to the people you talk to. I probably read the books you didn't, because you were too busy working on your sales pitch, or curating your posse.

So there you are again, giving some of yourself so you can take much more in return. Exploit the resources, the good-will, the gullibility and pain of others. Voluntary, cheap labor, free software, free licenses, free content and free beer. Sometimes you'll pay, sometimes I'll pay, but we gain nothing other than a few laughs and some bruised, hypersensitive, needy egos. I have to wonder if you ever built anything of note yourself. I can't tell anymore what's honest about you and what's dishonest. What's real and what's pretence. You'll find a cause that will serve your needs, you'll grab it and run with it to investors, conferences, seminars, work-shops, roundtables, parties, art galleries, hackerspaces, incubators... anywhere you can sell the cause and find believers in something you don't believe in yourself.

Because if you did, you'd be fucking serious about it. You'd give up that bullshit venture capitalist mentality that's there to make money for the few and feed your ego in the process. You'd see how it's all exploitative and stupid, and then you'd be truly embarrassed. Very embarrassed. You would understand that when you ask me to join an effort being made in the name of a cause I strongly believe in, and then you make a mockery of that effort, I feel stupid for even trying. And then I'm angry. So angry that I may say nothing, out of respect for those around us who are truly trying to make something of the moment, not only for themselves but also for others – like Bassel, who has sacrificed so much for something he believed in, with nothing in it for himself. Instead, I'll pour my anger and disappointment here. And my love. Because without love, I wouldn't have cared to write this. Without hope that you will read this and have a "FUCK ME!" moment, I wouldn't have bothered. Because you're awesome. And you're so full of shit.

"FREEDOM TO" VS. "FREEDOM FROM"

Martin Paul Eve

Unlike Bassel Khartabil, the cost to me, personally, of my free-knowledge work has been cheap. I have not paid with my freedom. In fact, I have been incredibly privileged to have conducted my work in creating free and open systems for the dissemination of scholarly knowledge in a geographical space (the UK and the British university) and political time that for the most part actually rewards such undertakings. If I say there is a cost, I feel it is a difference almost of type by comparison, rather than of degree, with respect to the price that Bassel has already paid.

But there is still some way to go, even in my privileged world. For the most part, academics are assessed on their publication record in a recognised disciplinary space, publishing with known proprietary publishers. There are very few positions available for the practical implementation of change in the academy (praxis). This is so to the extent that Kathleen Fitzpatrick, a fully tenured professor in the States, quit her post to work on publishing initiatives at the Modern Languages Association. Fitzpatrick wrote: "This is of course not to say that one can't change the world from inside the protections of tenure. But I do think that those protections often encourage a certain kind of caution, certainly in the process of obtaining them, and frequently continuing long after, that works against the kinds of calculated risk that a chance like this requires."

Even in my own academic publishing, though, there is a double bind. Many of my colleagues continue to find (or at least believe) themselves torn between publishing openly and having a career in the university. Dissemination and assessment find themselves in conflict because proprietary publishers own most of the venues for academic dissemination. And hiring panels look for the books published by the brands whose quality-control procedures they trust. But if those procedures and trusted systems are owned by entities whose business models depend on selling commissioned copies, then despite the fact that academics can give away their work (because they have a salary) this knowledge will remain imprisoned.

Even worse, this coercion (as I see it) to publish in known brand and usually-proprietary venues as a proxy for hiring in the university is defended as academic freedom (the freedom to choose to publish where one wants, rather than being told to publish openly). Certainly, it's done by "soft power" and a reputational/symbolic economy, but I did not feel free when I had to publish my first book with a commercial press. I'm still grateful to them because I needed the book for my job. They did good work on it and I can't fault the people who helped me there. But few people can actually read that book now because it is so expensive. I signed away the copyright as the price for a job. In an ideal world, I would have published this openly.

So, even as individuals (such as Bassel) fight for their true personal freedom that was taken away because they developed open-source software and facilitated freedom of expression, people around me continue to claim that it should be their right to lock knowledge away and that this is a freedom for them (see Cary Nelson's article in Inside Higher Ed. for an example). I do not think it should be. Academic freedom in its real and proper definitional sense is important (the right to speak truth to power) but we should not demean it by saying that it is about one's right to lock knowledge away from those who cannot pay.

When I say things like this, I am told I am anarchistic, that I want to destroy tradition, and that I am somehow an enemy of quality in academia. I have also been told

that this coercive soft-power structure of proprietary publishing doesn't even exist (usually by people who haven't
tried to get an academic job in the last decade). It does
exist, and I am not trying to destroy academic publishing.
I am trying to make academia and academic publishing the
altruistic spaces of knowledge-sharing that they should be.
As academics, giving people worldwide the freedom to read
our work should always take precedence over our personal
benefit from publishing in closed venues. I have not always
been able to negotiate this cost successfully so far, but I will
not defend my self-interest as a "freedom" when there are
people who have really lost their freedom for this cause.

FREE CULTURE IN AN EXPENSIVE WORLD

Shauna Gordon-McKeon

"Free as in speech, not free as in beer."

How many times have you heard this explanation of free software? It's cute, catchy, and a little too glib. After all, nothing's ever that simple. But this phrase is more than an oversimplification – it's a misleading metaphor, and it represents a fundamental oversight of the free culture movement.

"Speech" and "beer" – the choice of metaphors is telling. When we compare free software to free speech, we cast it as a natural right based on liberty, rather than a legal right based on property. This is quite agreeable to US Americans,[3] especially the techno-libertarian set. We adore free speech, the most popular part of our first and favorite amendment. Free beer, on the other hand, is a harder metaphor to swallow. But the focus on speech, on liberty-based rights, does not dispel the implications for property rights, only obscures them. Let's take a closer look.

While the first and second freedoms in the Free Software Definition are arguably matters of liberty, the third and fourth require the creator to let users distribute copies, and modified copies, of their software. To use a Free Culture license, as defined by Creative Commons, one must similarly agree to allow adaptations of one's work for commercial purposes. These licenses echo the demand of open scientists for access to the experimental methods and results of other researchers, and the insistence of music sharers and fanficcers in copying, modifying, and remixing the media they love.

---

[3] I am from the United States. This essay is written from that limited perspective, and may not apply to other countries and cultures.

It's clear that developers, researchers, musicians and writers create something of value. The free culture movement exhorts them to give that value away. We say it's a matter of liberty, but mainstream culture takes a different perspective, focusing instead on "intellectual property." Free culture advocates often reject the idea of intellectual property, arguing that digital products, unlike food or cabinets or cars, may be trivially copied. One can produce a thousand copies of Emacs, or of Harry Potter, in a literal second. Without scarcity, there's no need for property.

But scarcity is not a natural phenomenon, determined entirely by what is technologically possible. Like so many things, it is socially constructed. Humanity produces enough food to feed the world, enough vaccine to wipe out a dozen diseases, and, in the United States at least, enough housing to shelter our six hundred thousand homeless brothers and sisters. Why should we direct our energies against artificial scarcity in culture, when artificial scarcity elsewhere causes more fundamental harm?

It's not surprising then that so many members of the free culture movement are, like myself, immensely privileged. As the child of an upper middle-class family, a United States citizen, a white, cis college graduate, I have no fear that I will ever be hungry, homeless, or without vital health care. Without persistent reminders of these artificial scarcities, it is easy for me to focus on free culture; I can ignore property because I have access to plenty of it.

Like many other free software activists, I have used the phrase "free as in speech, not free as in beer" for years. But I have come to understand that it is not an explanation but an equivocation. Free culture absolutely has implications for property, and we need to face them.

The schism between Free Software and Open Source Software can be interpreted through the response to this problem. Free Software advocates tend to embrace liberty rights, preferring not to think about property, and often eschewing the idea of intellectual property altogether (while retaining, for the most part, their belief in other kinds of property). Open Source advocates, on the other hand, try to reconcile the property implications of free software with the capitalist culture in which most of it is produced. Open source, they argue, will increases the value of your property. As Mako Hill notes in his essay *When Free Software Isn't Better*,[4] the Open Source Initiative's mission statement focuses on the higher quality and lower cost of open source software. But, he continues, free/open source software is sometimes of lower quality and lower value to individuals and businesses. The reconciliation of free software and capitalist culture, always fragile, falls apart.

But the open source approach is not the only way to come at "free as in beer". The private capital of businesses using open source isn't the only kind of property. There is – and always has been – the commons.

It is easy to reframe the arguments for free culture around the commons. The case for open science becomes the case for public knowledge. The case for free distribution of art and literature becomes the case for shared culture. And the case for free software becomes the case for collectively built, collectively-evaluated technology. Free culture, then, is a movement which advocates universal access to a common good.

This is not a new perspective, of course. One of the most well-known free culture organizations, Creative Commons, uses precisely this framing. But many others reject it, and even those who embrace a digital commons often ignore the pressing threats to our natural and social commons. They advocate for free culture but not for public education, uni-

---

[4]https://mako.cc/writing/hill-when_free_software_isnt_better.html

versal health care, guaranteed housing, and basic income, or their equivalents

This is not just a matter of morality. The lack of a fiercely protected natural and social commons endangers the digital one. In a scarcity society, our labor must be hoarded jealously. People don't have time to learn about their computers, submit patches to projects, seek out free music instead of stolen music. They don't have the security to publish in open access journals, to protest surveillance, to give away their art or their software in hope of future reward. Many who would love to participate in free culture cannot, as Ashe Dryden lays out eloquently in her piece *The Ethics of Unpaid Labor and the OSS Community*.[5] Like unpaid political and literary internships, free software contributions act as a filter, allowing only the privileged to participate.

It's tempting to wave away this last issue by arguing that less privileged people have greater access to free culture than to proprietary cultural products. After all, we're giving it away! But accessibility is seldom a priority in free culture – in free software, many projects are made for other developers and we celebrate "scratching your own itch". Not that a focus on less privileged people is always better – in fact, it can be deeply condescending and unhelpful. No, these arguments miss the point entirely. The groups underrepresented in free culture are not hamstrung primarily by lack of access to the digital commons, but by threats to the natural and social commons.

Acting in solidarity with the struggle for physical security and against abuse is not only the right thing to do, it benefits all of us. When the free culture movement represents the fullness of human diversity, scratching your own

---

[5]http://www.ashedryden.com/blog/the-ethics-of-unpaid-labor-and-the-oss-community

itch will leave everyone satisfied. When it contains everyone who shares its values, we'll have the resources and the reach we need to ensure a vibrant and widely-treasured digital commons.

We live in alarming times. Even the computers with which we create these digital gifts are made, too often, by people trapped in abusive conditions, using processes that blight our primal Commons, the global environment. We cannot abstract away these facts; we cannot advocate for free culture as though in a vacuum. We must advocate for the commons in all of its forms – digital, social, economic, environmental – before the cost of freedom becomes too high to bear.

WHAT IS OPEN?

Richard Goodman

After looking at "Open is not a License", I decided to take a look at some of the definitions of the noun "open" in the dictionary, and was inspired to write a short poem around what "open" might mean to people. This poem is dedicated to my own poetry inspiration, my father Don Goodman, who passed away in March 2015 at the age of 75.

What is open? Is it a gap or a space? Is it something in public? Or a practice we chase?

Open is unenclosed It is an expanse Did we get here by planning? Or merely by chance?

Open is an opportunity A chance to broaden the mind Free tools and resources To benefit all of mankind

Open is an aperture Something you look through Access for all Not just the few

Open is a cavern A vast empty space A new way of working Falling into place

Open is a competition That anyone can enter A growing global movement With sharing at its centre

THE OPEN WORLD

Lorna Campbell

In *Open is not a License*[6] Adam Hyde has described openness as 'a set of values by which you live...a way of life, or perhaps a way of growing, an often painful path where we challenge our own value system against itself.'

To my mind, openness is also contradictory. I don't mean contradictory in terms of the polar dichotomy of open vs. closed, or the endless debates that seek to define the semantics of open. I mean contradictory on a more personal level; openness raises contradictions within ourselves. Openness can lead us to question our position in the world; our position in relation to real and perceived boundaries imposed from without and carefully constructed from within.

In one way or another I have worked in the open education space for a decade now. I have contributed to open standards, created open educational resources, developed open policy, written open books,[7] participated in open knowledge initiatives, facilitated open events, I endeavour to be an 'open practitioner', I run a blog called Open World.[8] However, I am not by nature a very open person; my inclination is always to remain closed. I have had to learn openness and I'm not sure I'm very good at it yet. It's a continual learning experience. Openness is a process that requires practice and perseverance. (Though sometimes circumstances leave us with little choice, sometimes it's open or nothing.)

---

[6]Hyde, A., (2015), Open is not a license, `http://www.adamhyde.net/open-is-not-a-license/`

[7]Thomas, A., Campbell, L.M., Barker, P., and Hawksey, M., (2012), Into the Wild – Technology for open educational resources, `http://publications.cetis.org.uk/2012/601`

[8]Open World, `https://lornamcampbell.wordpress.com/`

And of course, there is a cost; openness requires a little courage. When we step, or are pushed, outside our boundaries and institutions, it's easy to feel disoriented and insecure. The open world can be a challenging and unsettling place and it's easy to understand the impulse to withdraw, to seek the security of the familiar.

When large scale open education funding programmes first started to appear, (what an impossible luxury that seems like now), they were met with more than a little scepticism. When a major OER funding initiative was launched in the UK in 2009,[9] the initial response was incredulity.[10] Surely projects weren't expected to share their resource with everyone? Surely UK Higher Education resources should only be shared with other UK Higher Education institutions? It took patience and persistence to convince colleagues that yes, open really did mean open, open for everyone everywhere, not just open for a select few. One perceptive colleague at the time described this attitude as 'the agoraphobia of openness'.[11]

Although open licences and open educational resources are more familiar concepts now, there is still a degree of reticence. An undercurrent of anxiety persists that discourages us from sharing our educational resources, and reusing resources shared by others. There is a fear that by opening up our resources and our practice, we will also open ourselves up to criticism, that we will be judged and found wanting. Imposter syndrome is a real thing; even experienced teachers may fail to recognise their own work as being genuinely innovative and creative. At the same time, openness can

[9]UKOER, https://www.jisc.ac.uk/rd/projects/open-education

[10]Campbell, L.M., (2009), OER Programme Myths, http://blogs.cetis.org.uk/lmc/2009/05/20/oer-programme-myths/

[11]I cannot remember who said this, but the comment has always stayed with me.

invoke a fear of loss; loss of control, loss of agency, and in some cases even loss of livelihood. Viewed through this lens, the distinction between openness and exposure blurs.

But despite these costs and contradictions, I do believe there is inherently personal and public value in openness. I believe there is huge creative potential in openness and I believe we have a moral and ethical responsibility to open access to publicly funded educational resources. Yes, there are costs, but they are far outweighed by the benefits of open. Open education practice and open educational resources have the potential to expand access to education, widen participation, and create new opportunities while at the same time supporting social inclusion, and creating a culture of collaboration and sharing. There are other more intangible, though no less important, benefits of open. Focusing on simple cost-benefit analysis models neglects the creative, fun and serendipitous aspects of openness and, ultimately, this is what keeps us learning.

In the domain of knowledge representation, the Open World Assumption 'codifies the informal notion that in general no single agent or observer has complete knowledge'[12]. It's a useful assumption to bear in mind; our knowledge will never be complete, what better motivation to keep learning? But the Open World of my blog title doesn't come from the domain of knowledge representation; it comes from the Scottish poet Kenneth White[13], Chair of 20th Century Poetics at Paris-Sorbonne, 1983-1996, and a writer for whom openness is an enduring and inspiring theme. White is also the founder of the International Institute of Geopoetics[14],

---

[12]Open World Assumption, https://en.wikipedia.org/wiki/Open-world_assumption

[13]White, K., (2003), Open World. The Collected Poems, 1960 – 2000, Polygon.

[14]International Institute of Geopoetics, http://institut-geopoetique.org/en

which is 'concerned, fundamentally, with a relationship to the earth and with the opening of a world'[15]. In the words of White:

no art can touch it; the mind can only try to become attuned to it to become quiet, and space itself out, to become open and still, unworlded[16]

---

[15]White, K., (2004), Geopoetics: place, culture, world, Alba.
[16]White, K., (2004), 'A High Blue Day on Scalpay' in Open World. The Collected Poems, 1960 – 2000, Polygon.

COSTS OF OPENNESS

Tim Boykett

This is a collection of notes about some thoughts on openness as a way of working, living and acting. The summary might be that openness is about conversations, about being able to discuss things, about not sticking to your guns about taste, correctness, relevance and all that, but about building communities of sharing, caring and being able to correct one another's mistakes. Maybe openness is a state, not a statement; a process, not a proclamation.

We do not do copyright every well at Time's Up: "Copyright is problematic. Contact for clarification" or something similar is at the bottom of many of our web pages. We do not think we can make a single licence statement that will work. We would like to talk to people and organisations about what they would like to do with the images, the texts, the audio files. We were surprised when a huge image from our work was used to announce the application for Linz to become the European Capital of Culture, without asking us. It is nice to be so appreciated that we are a beacon of Linz culture, but we ask you to talk to us. A licence is possibly a way to avoid talking to one another, openness is perhaps about encouraging us to talk, to think, to share and communicate, not just announce.

Open academic publishing allows too much nonsense and badly written yet often useful stuff to get out. Peer review does not stop this, but quality reviewing does. This is a discussion between the author(s) and someone who cares. A reviewer is a peer who should care. If one is asked to be a reviewer, it is bound up with some work and some responsibility. It is not a job of letting your friends in and keeping your foes out. It is a job and responsibility, one of the rights and responsibilities that comes along with the context of being part of the academic or research community. It is possible to say "either this is badly written, or I do not care enough about it to develop an opinion" as a way to pass on the chalice. If no reviewer can be found who cares about the work, then perhaps no one cares about it at all and perhaps it is not worth publishing. Peer review means that the question of "who are your peers?" needs to be answered. Who are they really? Who cares? This is not about advertising or selling your work, about making people care, but about finding out who does. I do not have the right to demand that you care about my work. You cannot keep up with all the things that you might be interested in, so unless you can trust that I have made something that you care about, why would you bother looking at it?

Less is more. Fewer things to sort through. We have too many books, publications, articles, white papers, etc, etc: how to find what we need, let people know about what we do. We in the sense of all the communities I am involved in, from Time's Up through the universities, the research communities, the cultural communities and the world in general. Not all forms of openness can help that, many will harm it.

Patents only help if you want to "exploit" the invention. If you just care about doing interesting things, then being first is enough. Or even just doing it. Patents have that secondary effect, that once the idea is patented, we can all see how it works. So Patents are opening and closing: I know how it works, but I cannot copy it commercially. Like open source software: I was surprised to learn that commercial programmers are not allowed to look at how something is coded in open source software, in case they accidentally copy the programming technique. So for them, making it open closes it. There is, of course, the danger of reinventing the wheel (we have done that), wasted effort, dead-end developments. That's fine. In the long run, we are all dead and all the effort was futile. But in the meantime, let's keep it interesting. Let's share ideas and experiences and find communities to be involved in.

Open acknowledges mistakes and wrong directions. But we don't need to proclaim them: the reason there is little interest in the "Journal of Negative Results" is that failure often just means "I cannot see how to do this" rather than the implied, or even believed "this cannot happen." Mathematics is a great place to investigate this. A naive mathematician will say that something is obvious because they cannot imagine why it cannot be true (and will use that as an argument!). This might often be true, but it is not an argument. This is an enunciation of "common sense" or "intuition" and mathematics is a machine for breaking intuition. By doing the details, you might find out why the statement is false. Or why it is true, not just because there is no option, but because of something more interesting and useful. Mathematics is about this openness in all its horrible, gory, intricate detail. A mathematical paper is filled with long proofs because these are the things that interrupt or confirm beliefs, hopes, steps to results that are interesting. Openness here means that I open up my mind and show you not only that I can do this thing, but how I do it, so that you know that each time I do it, the answer is true. And thus you can do it too. It is open and open.

In order to be relevant, mathematics needs two things: to be true and to be interesting. One of the downsides of open publishing is that spotting the interesting becomes harder, because there are no gatekeepers who polish, edit, review and perhaps reject the ugly dross. We have to use coding as a gatekeeper. Spotting references to Einstein, especially how he is wrong, lets us know that a physics paper is probably pseudoscience. The formatting of LaTeX as an indicator of seriousness, Microsoft Word as a sign of an enthusiastic but probably misguided amateur. But these codes are false, and occasionally as false as James Lovelock's issues with scientific publishing from outside an institution: because his address was not a university or company, journals rejected his papers. Discussions were had and his papers were accepted, but it was more effort, there was a gatekeeper that was using inappropriate codes.

Openness has so many other branches. Money earnt, work done, distractions allowed. In collective work, we often agree upon a "basic wage" and share the work equally, something like from each according to their abilities, to each according to their needs. But how many innovators are independently wealthy and don't really need any financial help? How many have artists have a side job as advertisers or share brokers? Drunken writers write about drinking, not about what they do to actually pay the bar tab and postage for their manuscripts. Academics have tenure to allow them to undertake long projects. Or stay at home. Or start a business. Or hide, tutor school kids, write a science communication novel or a million other things. Are these distractions, or are they desired tangential outcomes? Do we need transparency here to know what is going on? Or does that break trust? How much box-ticking and metric analysis is needed to ensure that "public monies" are being correctly spent on science, humanities, culture and the arts? Are the numerical results of bums on seats and webpage views actually useful, or is that just another coded gatekeeper? If you can get through the dross of the application, then you are serious enough to be able to make it happen.

Perhaps transparency breaks trust. Perhaps openness creates not just abundance but waste. In the sense of "There's no such thing as waste, just stuff in the wrong place." It is probably worth keeping a lot of things out of the public eye, of not sharing every little detail on a blog or a series of explanations of your theory of everything, or your theory of everything else. Who are your peers, who are your colleagues? If you have a question or a new idea, formulate it properly. You might find the answer yourself while formulating it (Oh, that's what I meant!), you might realise that the idea breaks once it is communicated or becomes trivial (Ah, there are none of those to worry about). Then talk to your colleagues, your community, the people who know you and can help get over the first hurdles. Only then is it worth taking your idea to a larger group, your peers. StackExchange and other places are filled with comments that a given question is a duplicate of a given question, that the questioner is wasting time and space by not doing their research. If I want you to invest time in reading my question, you need to trust me that I have bothered answering the question already. That I have looked in all the normal places, tried the standard solutions. If I want to revolutionise gender theory, then I need to have read enough background, not just thought about it a bit and been excited by an idea.

Paul Erdos is an acclaimed mathematician, who would arrive with the statement "my brain is open" and work with colleagues on problems before travelling onwards to the next stop on his never ending journey. This openness led to him being the most published mathematician in history. His case is rare. The web is filled with examples of extremely smart, well-meaning people sharing their complex and intricate examinations of ways to improve the world, from engineering systems science analyses of climate issues to disaster relief planning. However, the absolute openness of their sharing means that every idea that crosses their well-fed minds gets deposited in the collection, pages of PDFs, hundreds of blog posts, hours of video lectures: too much! It is said that mathematicians are cheap. They require paper, pens and a large wastepaper basket. This process of disposal, of winnowing out the dross and keeping the good stuff, is the core of good work. If only I would learn that myself.

MY BRAIN ON FREEDOM

Mike Linksvayer

A cost of participation in free knowledge movements is "stupidity" – an assault on intelligence, wisdom, reason, knowledge. The net effect of free knowledge on intelligence is probably positive, possibly hugely positive if free knowledge movements succeed in thoroughly commoning the noosphere, making collaboration and inclusion the dominant paradigm for all economically valuable knowledge production and distribution. But the stupidity costs of free knowledge are real and painful, at least to me. Fortunately the costs, if acknowledged, can be decreased, and doing so will increase the chances of achieving free knowledge world liberation.

I want to explore briefly how individuals, communities, and society are affected by various kinds of costs of free knowledge. This is going to be cursory and incomplete. Very possibly also stupid: my mind has been infected by free knowledge for about 25 years.

Commitment makes us morally stupid, lazy, and unconvincing. Claiming that knowledge freedom is a moral issue is not a valid moral argument, but merely an unsupported claim which ought be embarrassing if not immediately followed or preceded by justification and more importantly, critique of said justification. This is not to praise people who claim that freedom (or openness) is a matter of efficiency rather than morality – they haven't avoided making a moral claim. Moral claims about freedom and efficiency as top values have been relentlessly scrutinized by moral philosophers and social scientists. Still there is much more to say. Free knowledge movements probably have much to contribute to the discourse, but we have to stop being satisfied with straw man arguments and propaganda, even while acknowledging that such have a place. Paths forward include breaking down and scrutinizing "free as in freedom" from the perspectives of various conceptions of freedom and other values and objectives such as efficiency, equality, and security. Doing so will make you morally smarter, more interesting, and make it more possible for people and movements with non-freedom top goals or different conceptions of freedom to join in the struggle for free knowledge.

Opportunity cost. Participating in free knowledge movements often entails filling one's brain with ridiculous trivia (e.g., about copyright), developing one's skills to workaround underdeveloped systems and institutions (e.g., administering one's own server, [self-]publishing with little or no support for financials, distribution, marketing), and self-exclusion from dominant venues and tools. Each of these has a huge cost. You could be learning something non-ridiculous, developing capabilities and competitive advantage rather than engaging in a brutal exercise of de-specialization. One step forward is to admit that these are huge costs, take them on carefully, and avoid criticizing those who fail to fail to take them on, at least not without acknowledging that they are costs rather than, or at least in addition to being moral imperatives. Once admitted, free knowledge movement actors might prioritize reducing these costs.

Scale. Free knowledge movements are often thought of as "bottom up" – see phrases such as "many eyes make bugs shallow" and "democratized innovation", the idealization of DIY, decentralization, and contribution by individuals and small non-profits; and suspicion of huge government and companies – at best dominant institutions can be "hacked." Now DIY and bottom up innovation and small non-profits are vital and cool (well maybe small non-profits are only vital) – but alone, they are dwarfish and stupid. Huge systems and organizations are not only corrupt and unjust – they have huge economies of scale, deep and specialized knowledge, and win markets and wars. Small scale free knowledge actors are foragers who feel comfortable among their kin and kindred, fearful of the farmers and their kings and armies – and are about to (on the scale of human history) be driven to extinction. If freedom is important, freedom movements abhorring large institutions is the ultimate stupidity. The path forward is clear – the handful of already sizable free knowledge organizations such as Wikimedia, Mozilla, and Red Hat must get much larger, entrepreneurs ("social" or "for-profit") attempting to create more free knowledge "unicorns" (we can count consumer surplus and other social values in the "billions" evaluation) encouraged, and sights set on taking the commanding heights (e.g., mandating free knowledge through procurement and regulation) rather than voluntary marginalization and hacks. One conception of a stupid person or movement is one that consistently fails to meet its stated goals, or consistently is outperformed by its competition, effectively taking two steps back for every one forward, with bonus for failing to realize this is what is happening. In this sense dwarfish free knowledge actors are stupid, and will remain so until they crack the logic of collective action, mostly through huge free knowledge institutions, though other improved coordination mechanisms may help as well.

Diversity. Free knowledge movements aren't very diverse, which contributes mightily to the costs of joining and scaling, and thus intelligence, in addition to missing out on intelligence benefits of diverse perspectives documented elsewhere. Much has been written about lack of diversity in free knowledge movements, and there is currently considerable effort by various actors to increase diversity, so let me re-confirm my biases; that is, make additional suggestions. Moral certainty is bad for diversity. It is repulsive on its face, but also allows continuing failure to make free knowledge concerns pertinent to more diverse groups. Huge opportunity costs make participation feasible only for the relatively privileged, self-limiting diversity. Lack of scale makes free knowledge movements insular and non-diverse. Like hanging out with culturally similar committed free knowledge hacks? Great, you're in the right social club. Want world liberation? The cost in the short term might be shedding some certainty, insularity, and fear, and thus feeling stupid. It'll make you, me, and free knowledge movements much smarter in the longer term.

Toxin. One topic endemic to most free knowledge movements is worth calling out as an especially potent brain toxin: licenses. Yes they're necessary for the most part given bad default knowledge governance. But they make us stupid, over and above knowledge of copyright, patent, and other regimes entailed. Identities are wrapped up in particular license preferences. Consequential claims of license effects are strenuously argued with zero evidence. No worked-out model, no empirical evidence, whether from economics lab or natural (possibly instigated) experiments. Anyone looking at these debates from the outside (unfortunately almost nobody does so we're spared the richly deserved embarrassment) ought to laugh at the level of evidence freedom observed. Emphasis on licenses is morally ruinous. Developers, authors, etc. are placed in a privileged position: supposedly freedom is the right of all, but creator choice is lionized. The consequences are terrible too: creator choice is a recipe for dwarfism. Licenses are a distraction as well from public policy. Acknowledging again that licenses are necessary, the step forward seems obvious: re-conceptualize licenses away from vehicles of creator choice towards prototypes for commons-favoring public policy. This exercise and actualization will make free knowledge movement actors much smarter – we'll have to engage with the non-dwarfish implications of free knowledge and actually convince people with other top policy concerns rather than hide from them.

One way to decrease the stupidity of free knowledge movements is more cross-fertilization and knowledge and tool sharing across said movements. Stupid-making knowledge acquisition about topics such as copyright and licenses ought not need to be re-experienced in each free knowledge movement silo. Intelligence-building comprehensive criticism also ought be shared across silos. Breaking apart the silos would also increase diversity – each has a different mix of participants, even if they are also almost all biased in some of the same ways. While good for the whole, a warning to individuals: attempting to learn about and cross-fertilize multiple free knowledge movements might come at an extra high cost to your intelligence.

TOO POOR NOT TO CARE

Ben Dablo

I am writing about free culture from the perspective of someone who uses free software and consumes free culture because it's the only thing I can afford. Although I pay a heavy opportunity cost, the alternative is supporting proprietary regimes that are actively making the world worse.

At the risk of my future social and economic mobility, I have a confession to make: I don't have much money. I'm one minor disaster from being completely reliant on the generosity of others again. Poor is the common way of putting it, but I try to avoid self-labeling as such since that would invite further disadvantage. Why I don't have money is a personally well-trodden topic, but for many reasons I won't discuss, it's a common state for many people. Despite having little capital in a society that places so much emphasis on capital, I consider myself fortunate.

I have the privilege of writing these words using free software on a (mostly) free operating system. My computer isn't even modern enough to run a currently supported proprietary OS. Much of my education and character can be traced back to free culture sources. The novel "Down and Out in the Magic Kingdom", by Cory Doctorow, introduced me to a world where the alternatives to closed systems could win, where one could even thrive without the motivation of securing as much private ownership and IP as possible. It was released under a Creative Commons non-commercial license that inspired me to write, freed from the assumption that I must always choose between success and my principled opposition to proprietary regimes.

That's how I felt over ten years ago as a student, but a decade on, I wonder if the cost has been worth it. Perhaps

I'd be financially secure if I went with Microsoft products in the developer space instead of the LAMP stack. Maybe I'd be a successful musician if I had spent my meager funds on proprietary music production software instead of struggling with free software packages that were often incomplete by comparison. Of course, all my unrealized potential could simply be attributed to my own shortcomings as a developer, musician, and writer. But what about everyone else, the young people that may someday be asked to choose between free culture values and success?

I would tell them without regret that I would choose the same path. Success at the price of one's principles is really an ethical failure framed the wrong way. In the past such a statement could be interpreted as melodrama; being forced to pay a small fee to consume old entertainment media is hardly the most pressing issue, but today the costs of closed systems and proprietary regimes are plainly manifest on a global scale. In the human rights space, free software contributors build tools used by dissidents, activists, and whistleblowers. Proprietary vendors, when they're not busy adding backdoors to their software at the behest of governments, largely ignore those groups. In the environmental space, free knowledge contributors make educational videos and texts freely available to millions, while traditional publishers print books on established topics that are bound from birth for the landfill as next year's edition will supersede this year's. Duplication of effort on a massive scale to get around someone else's intellectual property has become yet another unnecessary source of carbon emissions.

Freedom has many costs. It might even prevent you from ever being materially wealthy. However, sacrificing our ideals when so much external to ourselves depends on them is a cost we can no longer afford.

INSIDE OR OUTSIDE THE MOVEMENT

John Wilbanks

Working in the free knowledge movement may mean working in a space that is better fitted to contemporary technology, but it also means working against several dominant themes in contemporary society and regulation. Most of our societies prize fences, whether through copyright or patent or contract or just simple withholding of secrets. Investors prefer fences, and universities reward them too. As a result, working in free knowledge is often a fundamentally transgressive act, politically and economically. And transgression against dominant social concepts comes with so many different costs.

There's a cost to explain free knowledge, because it has to start with what's wrong with closed knowledge. That comes at a cost of having friends or family understand the job, with questions like "why do you keep working on this when you could make so much more money somewhere else?" There's a cost to always being the outlier in a "normal" room of professionals, working against the gravity that defines normal for everyone else. There's a cost in constantly looking for funding when the dominant capital systems don't reward or pay for freedom. There's a cost in always feeling weird, always feeling like the power systems want you to lose.

It's not unlike being in a startup religion, except there's actually evidence for the benefits of free knowledge.

There's also a cost within the movement, one we don't talk about much. When we do actually all get together, and for once we're not transgressing against the "rest of the people in the room," we have a nasty habit of judging each other, fighting each other over details that the rest of the

71

world doesn't even recognize. I've been guilty of this in the past. It's just so wonderful to be able to debate our work with others who agree with us that it's easy to get into the details, and all the passion we bring to changing the dominant social system suddenly is focused on those who we agree with the most.

This isn't an unusual cost. In fact, it's one of the most common costs of any social change movement. But it's the highest one, for me. The only advice I have is: we're in this together, those of us who care enough, those of us who see enough. It's easy to take that passion and turn it against ourselves, but that's a target that only helps the closed knowledge system maintain itself.

I've worked on recognizing that all of us, from the most strident backers of the public domain to those who embrace non-commercial licenses, from a total open commons to a network of managed commons, have way too much in common to subscribe to a purge mentality within free knowledge. I'm a lot less strict about applying definitions of freedom to people – those definitions are for knowledge objects! And I'm a lot more inclusive of different opinions within the free knowledge movement than I used to be. It means that at least I'm no longer paying the cost within the movement, and I'm reserving all the resources for the costs outside the movement.

FREEDOM AS A COMMODITY

Pete Ippel

Let's say freedom is a commodity not a dichotomy.

Therefore when considering the cost of freedom, I am inclined to compare use and exchange value. How does one quantify either? It's so very abstract. Is freedom useless? No. Freedom fulfills the human need to differentiate – to ascertain what makes someone or something different. Can one exchange freedom for something else? Yes, often for convenience, privacy, health, or safety. Freedom is not either/or, it's an absurd both/and of exchange and use value.

At this moment Bassel Khartabil is disappeared for communicating his views on freedom of expression and has been forced to exchange his freedom of mobility in addition to many other human rights. I stand with the #FREEBASSEL campaign in demanding Bassel Khartabil's location information and immediate release.

FREE AS IN COMMONS

hellekin

The Free Software Movement is 32 years old. In 1983, Dr. Richard Matthew Stallman, also known as rms, his computer user name, invited the world to write a sufficient body of free software to restore users' freedom, and for not having to use proprietary software ever. In his original announcement of the GNU system, on Thanksgiving, 1983, Stallman stated his reasons for building a complete operating system that would be entirely free software: sharing with others the programs you like, and to continue using computers without violating this, and other ethical principles.

Stallman was then working at the Artificial Intelligence laboratory of MIT, center of a substantial software-sharing community in the decades before. Hackers on PDP-10 computers there and in other places would write software and share it among themselves, as naturally as cooks share recipes. But in the early 1980s, the PDP-10 line of computers on which they had been writing software was discontinued. New architectures had appeared, such as VAX and 68020, that made most of their software obsolete. The operating systems on these new architectures, VMS and BSD UNIX, were encumbered with non-disclosure agreements. A program is like a recipe. A nonfree program is like a binary recipe that only your kitchen robot could make, but you couldn't reproduce yourself, nor share it with anyone else. Imagine going to a friend's house and enjoying a fantastic chocolate cake; when you'd ask for the recipe, they would tell you: "sorry dear, but I can't give it to you, only I am allowed to make it." How antisocial would that sound? That sounds exactly like nonfree software.

The software-sharing community at MIT's AI lab had collapsed the year before his decision, as most hackers went away to work at a new spin-off company. Stallman was faced with a stark moral choice: he could join the emerging proprietary software social system and close his eyes to the digital divide between developers and users; or he could leave the software industry altogether, but that would not prevent it from becoming antisocial; or he could, as his profession was to write operating systems, develop a new one that would protect the freedom to use, share, and improve software for all. He chose the latter, embarking onto the enormous project of creating an ethical world of software, starting with the GNU operating system, a system that would respect users' essential freedoms.

In an age of instant gratification, rarely the mind is put to measure the consequences of passing time. Hackers love to automate away the burden of repetition. To spread a political message, we need to repeat it; that's what rms has done for three decades. To establish freedom, we must teach many people to appreciate freedom. The tremendous achievements of software freedom to date don't end the need to remind people year after year that the struggle continues, even more importantly today.

The analysis has developed, but the original intent remains the same. In hindsight, free software advocates easily distinguish between individual and collective freedoms, to insist on the interdependence required to achieve our goal. But it took years to formalize the four essential freedoms and the free software definition.

The first two freedoms granted by free software to the user enable to run the software for any purpose, and to study how the software works to be able to adapt the source code to one's own needs. These freedoms enable each user to exert individual control over their computing. A programmer can learn from the source code. But not everyone is a developer and able to program software. Therefore, it was necessary to implement collective control of software, in the same way as for science and culture: to turn software into a commons. The other two freedoms enable sharing the code, that is the knowledge and know-how, with anyone so that you can help your neighbor, and being free to distribute modified versions of the software so that non-programmers can benefit from free software as well.

The four freedoms encourage synergies between users and developers for the benefit of all: a group of users can decide what to do; the programmers among them can implement it; If something scandalous is found in a free program, such as the malicious functionality commonly discovered in proprietary software, programmer-users will fix it and then distribute the corrected version widely to the other users.

Making changes though, is not always easy. All software is governed by copyright law, like many other creations such as text, photography, or video. When you distribute such works, the law grants you exclusive property over it, whether you like it or not: thus, if you release a program without taking a step to make it free, it is automatically nonfree. Copyright denies users the four freedoms by default. The step required to make a program free is to attach a legal statement, from the copyright holders, giving users the four freedoms. Such a statement is called a "free software license".

Free software licenses existed before 1983. Stallman's innovative legal hack, called "copyleft", was to write a copyright license, that required all copies redistributed, even modified, to come with the same freedoms. The GNU General Public License grants the four essential freedoms to everyone that gets a copy of the code, including any additions or changes, iteratively ad infinitem. It creates a community in which everyone gets freedom.

The essence of software freedom is control of your own

technology: the technology that you make, and the technology that you use. In a world dominated by software powerhouses, technology is often understood as the product created by inaccessible engineers and sold by their employing corporations. Whereas the users of a proprietary program are forcibly limited to being consumers, the users of free software are citizens of their software community and take part in the collective invention of technology. This prompts an incentive for cooperative research in computing, for the benefit of all humans, similarly to science, and culture.

Software, science, and culture have been under attack by promoters of so-called "Intellectual Property", a bag-word covering many different legal concepts with varying scopes, conveniently put together under a seemingly innocent umbrella that hides how different these laws are, and claims that human intellectual work comes solely from the mind of the person expressing it. It takes no effort to understand the deception here. A brief look into Greek mythology and the history of literature can easily demonstrate that, as Sir Isaac Newton famously wrote: even a genius sits on the shoulders of giants.

What are the issues with non-copyleft, or lax licenses, such the 3-clause BSD license?

Companies such as Apple want to convince you not to use copyleft on your software, because they would like to convert it into nonfree software and subjugate users with it. If you give them what they want, you may "have millions of users" but you will not have advanced their freedom at all. On the contrary, you would have chosen popularity over freedom, and lost technological sovereignty in the process.

Mac OS X is based on a BSD architecture. But FreeBSD hackers can't use what Apple built on top of their code that would benefit all their users. This is in essence the difference between copyleft and non-copyleft: the former insists the code remains free as it develops, including larger programs, while the latter encourages cannibalization of the source code by defectors.

How does that contrast with the GPL?

If Mac OS X was based on the GNU operating system, it would remain free. Copyleft is a cooperation enforcer, that respects their freedom to use our software, as part of our community; what it denies them is the chance to convert our software into an instrument to dominate others. The GPL is an institution to enable cooperation.

Defectors do not want to cooperate. They want to dominate others. Although they can use modified GPL software for their own interest in private, they refuse to become part of the community. The GPL requires that If they choose to distribute their modified version of the software, they must accept to become contributors to the software, like any previous contributors who enabled them to benefit from the program in the first place. They claim a (moral) right to abuse the work of others to make users divided and helpless.

It took Stallman a few years to clearly separate the two meanings of the English word "free". Free software is a matter of freedom, not price. Copies do not have to be gratis: you're free to offer copies in exchange for pay. But if the copies don't carry the four essential freedoms, they are not free software. The Latin root for liberty found in Roman languages gives a synonym to overcome the ambiguity of the English "free": libre. This allows us not to enter into a false debate regarding the alleged incompatibility of free software with commercial applications. If proprietary software vendors sell license rights to their users, free software vendors cannot do this; nevertheless they can still sell copies of the software, development itself, and services related to the it: distribution, support, education, etc.

There is a misleading simplification that consists in arguing that if the software source code is available, people won't pay to obtain it. But not everyone is a developer, and most people will prefer paying a company to take responsibility for their software: they do it all the time with proprietary software. The main difference with copyleft is that they don't pay copyleft free software vendors for a restrictive license: instead the license is there to protect them from abusive vendors!

In the USA, You can put a program explicitly in public domain. But that's equivalent to releasing it under a weak, pushover license. Doing so, however, falls back to the earlier case of a non-copyleft license: defectors can abuse your work and claim it for themselves. Making a program proprietary declares that anyone who goes there is under your power. Releasing it under a lax license declares that people there are free as long as they don't surrender that freedom to anyone else; the software is in the commons, precariously, as long as nobody privatizes it by making it nonfree. The choice of a copyleft free software license such as the GPL makes a stronger political claim: it tells the world you're willing to give away your work for others to build upon, as long as it irrevocably remains part of the commons, resisting others' attempts to pull it out.

ARCHITECTONICS
OF POWER

HACKING THE CONTRADICTIONS

Stéphanie Vidal

Contrary to most people's belief, contradictions are an interesting and powerful tool for the thinking process. They are something we often encounter in our minds. For some people, contradictions are the ultimate roadblock, whereas for others they are a just a stage of their reflection. The latter group, when realizing they are stuck with an insoluble confrontation, find the strength to make a sidestep in order to move forward.

With a twist, a bounce, an awkward move, they are able to overtake the contradiction, to hack it and go beyond.

We are at the edge of a critical moment where aporia are not only rhetorical, but contradictions are systemic.

Having a close look at the digital media fields, we find those contradictions at the core issues of contemporary productions such as art, critical design, literature, code, technology, philosophy, economy...

Most of them are seeking for disruptive technology, social innovation, philosophical renewal: they can be called a sidestep.

Maybe freedom of thought, to make and move, appears when we are able to make a sidestep Maybe freedom is just the possibility to take a sidestep Maybe freedom means the power for the people to stay in control of their dreams despite the reality of the system Maybe freedom is the way we ethically manage internal and external contradictions to go beyond.

TIME TO WAKE UP

Mushon Zer-Aviv

Freedom of information, much like freedom of markets, doesn't "naturally" lead to the kind of freedom we hope for in society. In fact, in the past decade since the rise of the free culture movement, we've seen many costs such as time, attention and education shifting to the side of content creators while financial profit is centralized by the data-hoarding Internet giants that enjoy the reputation of information liberators. Google, for example, is considered a great patron for free culture, whereas in practice it cannibalizes the free culture that it monetizes, offsetting the costs of culture from those consuming it, and profiting from those creating it, and that's us.

The technological principle that powers digital freedom of information, and that we celebrate through free culture and the creative explosion of the web, is the same technological principle that powers digital surveillance. We have to stop seeing these technological principles as "ready-made for culture" whether that be as a pre-made model for cultural exchange, or as a pre-made model for the end of privacy. This techno-determinism is a double-edged sword; it's time to wake up and realize that the new possibilities and challenges posed by digital networks should inform the way we decide to live our lives, not dictate it.

THE COST OF INTERNET FREEDOM

Geert Lovink

Dedicated to Bassel Khartabil, written for the Cost of Freedom Book Sprint.

Every act of rebellion expresses a nostalgia for innocence and an appeal to the essence of being." – Albert Camus

Let's translate Isaiah Berlin's "Two Concepts of Liberty" from 1958 to our age. Berlin distinguishes between negative and positive freedom: there is the negative goal of warding off interference, and the positive sense of the individual being his or her own master. In both cases, a fundamental distinction is made between the autonomy of the subject and the crushing reality of repressive systems. For Berlin, freedom is situated outside of the system. Written in the shadow of totalitarianism, at the height of the Cold War, there wasn't much else for him to expect. In that period, the notion of freedom as an everyday experience was absent. The existentialist gestures after World War II emphasized the legal rights of the individual-as-rebel who stood up against evil outside forces.

Right at the beginning of his famous essay, Berlin formulates Evgeny Morozov-type sentences that sound remarkably familiar to those involved in contemporary 'net criticism' debates.

"Where ends are agreed, the only questions left are those of means, and these are not political but technical, that is to say, capable of being settled by experts or machines, like arguments between engineers or doctors." And he continues: "That is why those who put their faith in some immense transforming phenomenon must believe that all political and moral problems can be turned into technological ones."

Berlin reminds us of the phrase of Friedrich Engels about "replacing the government of persons by the administration of things." Sounds very timely, no? But wait, is this an old communist phrase, or a libertarian dogma preached by Silicon Valley billionaires?

Fast forward ten or twenty years and the concept of 'the system' is no longer perceived as alien. In the 1970s, the idea spread that (computer) systems were man-made and could be programmed, designed, and thus democratized. The critique of the technocratic society that we can trace in the memories of Albert Speer, published in 1969, were soon to be forgotten and taken over by a fascination for the do-it-yourself spirit of the garage hackers. Instead of looking at IBM mainframe computers as a tool of 1984's Big Brother, the personal computer was introduced as a portable counter-cultural alternative, intended to undermine power as such and break it up into a 1001 fragments of decentralized, distributed expressions of human creativity.

Jump another thirty years onwards, and Internet free-dom activists run up against very clear boundaries and set-backs. Liberal obsessions with privacy and copyright are still interesting but no longer essential in order to under-stand the big picture. What's at stake is much larger than a bunch of legal issues, defined by lawyers. What's necessary is a comprehensive understanding of the political economy of the Net, combined with critical knowledge of global poli-tics. The legal strategies have run empty. It is now all about power politics and organization of the field. The loose ties that social media have left us with do not foster long-term collaborations but force us into a 24/7 cult of the update.

The philosophical question, can we find freedom inside the machine, should be answered with a definite no. So far, programmers, geeks and artists have stressed the possibili-ties of carving out small pockets for themselves, in order to realize their free software and creative commons projects. This 'temporary autonomous zones' approach has a liberal consensus as its premise, that the 'Internet' will tolerate such experiments within its infrastructure.

The original Internet freedom within the system is shrinking as we speak, and we lack the appropriate tools and strategies to do something to counter it. Soon we will be back at square one, demanding freedom of the Internet.

The ideal of freedom outside of the Matrix will not necessarily be Luddite in nature. The coming uprising against the Internet as a tool of surveillance and repression will be technologically informed, and needs to be distinguished from the related human right to have time off work and have a life. This ain't no offline romanticism. Our memes need to communicate this simple message: positive Internet freedom is the road to serfdom. We need to revolt against the soulless, mechanical ideas of the Silicon Valley engineering class and their solutionist marketing slogans. In order to prepare ourselves, we need an understanding of the Two Concepts of Internet Liberty.

WHY I CHOOSE PRIVACY

Sabrina Banes

This essay is adapted from one originally published on my personal website, missbananabiker.com.

I publish my work under my full name. I write about my life without holding back, except where innocent people might be harmed as a result of my writing about them.

You might wonder why I advocate so passionately for internet privacy when I tell the whole world all my secrets without restraint, when I am completely open about, for instance, being an abuse survivor who is this year celebrating my twentieth year of freedom.

1. I have always had the option of keeping my secrets. For years, while I was being abused, I was forced to keep secrets, and then I continued to do so because I was afraid of people's reactions to hearing about what I had survived.
   I personally don't care any more if you think I'm a weirdo because I am a weirdo, and I'm fine with that. In fact, my weirdness is what I have to offer the world.

2. So my weirdness and my truth are things I talk about because it's what I have to contribute, and because I'm tired of the forced silence which isolated me.

   Now I want to exercise my own free speech. I want to tell people about my experiences. I hope that maybe some of you will get ideas from all this for how to spark change in your own worlds, even if all you do is teach your kids that they have the right to establish firm boundaries. Particularly firm physical boundaries, like getting to decide who to hug and when.

3. But privacy is important. I have the right to be a private person if I choose to do so, and for about eighteen years I did choose to do so. I did that for my own safety. I have a right to preserve my own safety.

4. When it comes to the state spying on me, I admit I don't have much "to hide." There are things I would be a little embarrassed to know about if you learned them, but for me personally at this moment in time, concentrated state surveillance is not my biggest fear.

5. I personally am more afraid of all the trackers from Facebook and Amazon and other companies with which I do business. And that's why I flush my cookies with the frequency of a true paranoiac and use all sorts of browser extensions to protect myself to whatever degree I can.

6. But there are people, a lot of people, who have a genuine reason to fear state surveillance. I could easily be one of them. And I think it's important that you all read, for instance, about a really gross spying bill called CISA that passed the US Senate with only twenty-one votes against it. We are not fighting this spying. We are letting it happen.

7. Here's what Edward Snowden has to say about that bill: "What it allows is for the companies you interact with every day – visibly, like Facebook, or invisibly, like AT&T – to indiscriminately share private records about your interactions and activities with the government." Actually, the bill requires those companies to share your info with the NSA. Seriously.

8. Now you understand maybe why I am paranoid about my business-facing cookies.

9. If the government spies on citizens without our consent, without our knowledge, without valid reason, we all lose something precious. We lose the right to be flawed people. We all become criminals by default.

10. As an abuse survivor, I've lived under circumstances like that, where every move was monitored. And I have to tell you, living under a microscope is definitely not being free. When you have to account for every hour of your day to your abusive father, when you have to find places to hide contraband items like rock music cassettes, when you have to keep secrets as a matter of survival, you are not free.

    As a former preacher's daughter, I can tell you that I've also lived in a fishbowl, and fishbowls are not free places either. When your whole church discusses whether your parents are being profligate with their money by taking their thirteen-year-old daughter whose classmates call her "Bugs Bunny" to an orthodontist, that's not freedom.

11. As an army brat, I was raised to believe that the US government is some sort of heroic institution that exports freedom and democracy to the rest of the world. The first lessons I learned in my US Department of Defense school were about freedom and its importance.

12. Partly because I am an abuse survivor, I value justice. It's just super important to me that people be treated fairly and humanely and that their basic rights be respected.

13. I have always wanted the United States to be a nation that values freedom. I have always thought that

the most important line ever written by our founding fathers was not in the Constitution but in the Declaration of Independence: "...that all men are created equal, that they are endowed by their creator with certain inalienable rights, that among these are life, liberty and the pursuit of happiness."

14. With the spying, our government and others are taking our liberty and chilling our pursuit of happiness. By spying on us, they've put us in a position where we are constantly trying to cover our tracks. Even flushing your cookies is evidence you're suffering from a chilling effect. You shouldn't have to cover your tracks unless you're hiding from something.

15. This is also why you should be very, very worried about treaties like TPP, TTIP, and TiSA. The aforementioned spying bill, CISA, lays some of the groundwork in the US for those treaties, helps foster an environment that would allow the American government — and, with the treaties, corporations and governments around the world — to encroach on everyone's liberties even more.

16. As someone who has survived tyranny, the most important thing to me is never living under it again. As someone who is free with my opinions, it's important to me that I have the right to be free with my opinions.

17. Internet freedom is a women's issue. Have you read the 1972 Johnnie Tillmon piece from Ms. magazine, Welfare is a Women's Issue ? You should. It explains why access to food and shelter are vitally important to women.

18. Internet privacy is also vitally important to women. If your abusive partner has installed a keystroke logger on your computer, you have no freedom of association, expression or movement. To leave such a partner, a person would need to get to a computer at a public library or internet cafe, establish an anonymous identity, make private phone calls and check-in to a safe location without being tracked. The effect of one partner spying on another can be absolutely devastating, and the ability to escape such spying is crucial to survival.

    We need these tools to survive situations like the one above, situations which are all too common. People who want to make strong cryptography illegal, like FBI Director James Comey, are saying they don't want us to have the tools we need to in order to escape life-threatening situations. That's not just misguided; it's tyrannical and frightening. Comey is behaving like an abusive partner, trying to make some rule that you aren't allowed to stop him from reading all your emails and text messages. He and people like him are trying to make it illegal for people like me to survive this world.

19. The government and some of the bigger corporations have basically installed keystroke loggers on us, except they've done it in tricky ways we don't discover until after our privacy has already been compromised.

20. Edward Snowden recently said on Twitter, "Surveillance is not about safety. It's about power. It's about control."

You could replace the word "surveillance" with "abuse" and you'd have the same statement. This is why a free

Internet is so important to me. This is why the right to privacy is so fundamental in my opinion. Because we all deserve to be free from those who would hold us captive, whether those folks are abusers or stalkers or just the good people who've built a surveillance apparatus that makes the Stasi look like amateur hour.

We all deserve that freedom. Anyone who is a survivor should value that freedom, and anyone who has suffered oppression should viscerally understand why, and anyone who is human should do whatever they can to protect that freedom.

WHY I CHOOSE COPYRIGHT

Lucas Gonze

I used to have a peculiar habit: I went to great lengths to not infringe copyright. This was often misunderstood to be a statement in support of stronger copyright, taking Metallica's side against Napster.

My intention was different.

Engaging with a cultural product increases its value, regardless of whether the engagement produces immediate revenue. If you watch a movie, you help to give it cultural currency, meaning the kind of thing that is referenced in conversation.

If you watch a hit TV show and then talk about it, you make other people want it. If you sample it, you make other people want it.

This is regardless of whether infringement is involved. If you are never going to buy something, there is no loss of revenue when you don't pay. If no revenue is lost, then the holders of the copyright have benefited.

Why would I have to infringe to access the work? There might be a literal price (e.g. $20 for a CD) that was too high. Or the work might only be available on terms that I can't accept. For example, there might be DRM, or I might need a cable TV account. Those terms are a form of cost.

If I couldn't accept the price, and then infringement led me to help increase its value, I wouldn't be helping myself. If I refuse to engage at all,then I maximize the pressure I can exert on the vendor.

The vendor's ideal outcome is for me to pay the asking price. But the second best outcome, if I can't do that, is for me to help convince others to pay the asking price. The worst outcome is if I ignore the product.

I ignored products to create pressure on vendors to offer them on acceptable terms.

Purism was necessary. No doing what the copyright owner didn't want, even if I disagreed. No knowing infringement, no matter how absurd the implications.

No torrenting, Linux ISOs aside. No stream ripping. No DJ sets on Soundcloud. No singing Happy Birthday without a license.

Because by obeying the rules I could demonstrate why the rules need changing.

Evangelism didn't interest me, though. No preaching, no seeking converts. I just lived my life according to a dogma with only one adherent.

A more committed missionary would have done it differently because I could not have an impact this way.

What I was doing was a boycott. Boycotts rely on broad participation.

The people are not dogmatic, and they want torrents.

Over time, the vendors have gotten somewhat better. You can buy music without DRM. You can buy HBO a la carte, as HBO Now, without having to buy cable TV.

That was caused by market pressure. The masses are not purist, but they do prefer reasonable terms to ugly ones.

At the same time, my standards fell. The rise of mobile caused the computing experience to became so unfair, so centralized, so tightly controlled that my expectations with regard to media seem comically unrealistic. There's no chance of jail-broken phones becoming the stock experience.

When computing users have so much less power, holding out for more makes no sense.

Eventually, I softened my position to a more common one - pragmatism. I now avoid infringement, but will sometimes do it if the alternative is ridiculous. I now avoid ridiculous problems rather than seeking them out. It's a big change. It means that when the cost of media is too high, I will do my best to pay up anyway.

WHY I REFUSED MY PROPRIETARY SELF

Adam Hyde

I find myself, after all this time immersed in free culture, amazed at my holding on to some form of the proprietary way of thinking. Sometimes I have found myself consciously going quite a long way down that path before I stop myself and almost forcibly ask myself "hey! What are you doing?"

Some time ago I started a methodology called the Book Sprint. It's a way to facilitate the production of books in 3-5 days with a group of 6-12 people (or so). It took a long time to hammer out this method. Much financial, personal, and emotional pain to keep going down a road that nobody, including myself, really understood terribly well. Was it really possible to make it work? Well, it took about 4 years of hammering on this methodology, making plenty of mistakes, before I could actually think about it as a methodology. Before I could actually wield it with some form of embryonic artistry, see it in action, build upon it, improve it, teach it to others.

4 years is a long time. It felt like a long time. Truth is, I don't really know why I didn't give up, and my stubbornness is something that kind of shocks me, looking back.

Suddenly I could see the prospect of a sustainable lifestyle emerging. How would I make it happen and protect it? I had this horrible feeling that I was not good enough at scaling the project and some big ugly org with heaps of cash would scoop in and 'steal it'. I guess I meant they would swoop in and copy it. The danger of a ripped-off dream caught me off-guard and I went down the road of lawyers and trade mark protection for Book Sprints. This was my first step towards owning the methodology.

I look back at that now and I'm kind of amazed I went

down that path as far as I did. I didn't actually follow through with trade-marking. The lawyer told me it was going to cost more and more, and it gave me time to wake myself up. What was I doing? The fear of losing my creation led me down a blinkered "IP" way out of line with my personal politics. It brought me awareness to peel off the layers of proprietary living that transpires our skins.

The process is a process of painful personal growth. Sharing my experience with hardened free culture practitioners, I've met quick nods of agreement. Only the idealist newcomers look puzzled at my apparent failure: I'm not a true believer. There is no purity on the path to freedom. Walking through the shameful path of not meeting the high bar we've set ourselves to avoid proprietary life, I keep learning about how deeply embedded it is in our daily lives. I keep examining it and it keeps surprising me. I keep discarding it. There's still a long way to go.

Edited by hellekin, 3 Nov 2015, Pourrières, France.

IMAGE, IDENTITY, ATTRIBUTION, AUTHORSHIP

Christopher Adams

We can say that a photographer owns her images, in the same way that an author owns her words. (The shorthand for this ownership is copyright.)

However, we should not conclude that the photographer has rights to her subjects, legally or morally, in the same way that an author has rights to her ideas. The reason that a photographer cannot make claims upon her subjects is that her work crosses that boundary between persons, and persons have their own rights which must be considered.

We are not so ignorant as to say that a photograph will steal our soul, and yet we are dimly aware of a danger in pictures of our faces or bodies, as if something can be taken from us, and get away, to who knows what end. We know there could be a "cost" to each photograph that is taken.

Photography did not always enjoy the protections of copyright. The argument went that manipulating a machine (in this case, a camera), did not count as a creative act.

Eventually, the question of whether making a photograph rose to the level of authorship was settled by the courts, in the affirmative. Photographers are the authors of their creations and thus own the copyright.

That photographs are protected by copyright also means that a photographer is free to release her work under a free license that allows others to use, reproduce, modify, and learn from her creations. The minimal requirement to re-use a freely licensed photograph is the simple gesture of giving credit or attribution to the photographer, in the manner she specifies.

Free licenses apply to a photographer's rights as an author, and your rights as a user. However, they are silent on the legal and moral rights of the subjects of our photographs, which we might understand as the right of publicity.

In order to secure this additional right, the photographer must ask something of her subject.

The subject must consent not only to the photographer's use of his image, and to others' re-use and modifications of his image; he must also permit his name and identity to be associated with his image. That is the "cost" of the "freedom" of his picture. He lets a fragment of his soul escape out into the world, forever.

THE BURDEN OF JOURNALISM

Théophile Pillault

An Infinite and Unsolvable Debt

We practice journalism as we are in an age of working. However, after more than 15 years of reports and interviews, we are still not able to call it a job, because its cost has been so high in comparison with the rewards. High for our lives, precarious and submitted to media that don't even deserve our attention. High for the profession itself, which we happen to sometimes soil with doubtful deontological hygiene, or even worse, mimeticism.

Dealing with a less and less united journalism practice and even definition, reporters and information collectors are getting more and more individualistic. Journalism has always been a game for rich people, as many of them know, but it's getting dangerously worse as the job becomes more precarious, leading to an economic reign of division.

In France, the number of syndicated journalists is totally meaningless as they are thrown into a profession ruled by the publication race contest. For instance, less than a quarter of French registered photojournalists are members of a professional organization.

Journalism doesn't have the time any more to think itself through: reports follow each other at a rhythm the reader can't keep up with. And it doesn't really matter as they are all the same.

It seems that journalistic narration has been reduced to reporting on instabilities such as conflict geographies, financial markets mobility or multinational successfulness. For a few years, the Syrian battlefront seems to have become the only place for photojournalists to do their job. In France, mass-media contribution is limited to vox pops about arriving refugees or Greek debt. When it is not busy exploring gossip magazines, a massive part of specialized media just settles for streaming Facebook or Google citations.

In those conditions, it is hard to draw attention to celebrated Internet volunteer Bassel Khartabil, an open web developer who has been wrongfully detained in Syria since 15 March 2012. This prisoner stands at complicated crossroads between media and international stakes, and talking about his disappearance implies levels of analysis that the French media, it seems – if only they were the only ones – cannot handle. This fight for information, amongst other fights, struggles to make its way into newsrooms which look more and more like dominant system backrooms, left alone by any form of resistance.

As we face those ideological barriers, how can we hope to get more people outside those little circles already convinced to read dissident analyses?

Today, we still haven't found a satisfying setup to provide for the production and diffusion of chemically pure information, purified from political, institutional or personal stakes.

The same questions apply to online journalism. Neo-data journalists? Webdoc producers? Datavisualizers? They are under the same pressures as their paper ancestors. The Internet can't produce another type of mass information free from the rentability logics and industrial concentration that strikes the sector.

Sharing our analysis, dissidence or images in free information frameworks provides last victories for the small media people. But for how long? After 15 years of articles written on the edge, of unpaid reports, of lots of often spoiled written material, isn't it time to listen to reason and look for evidence? What would they say?

Maybe that this job doesn't exist or doesn't exist anymore.

However, very few societies can pretend to emancipate themselves without a free information system. So, we have to stand at the frontlines.

Because there is no cost for journalism or ideas, Bassel Khartabil is detained today, and other women and men will be. There is no cost of freedom. Just an infinite and unsolvable debt that nothing can resolve.

Let's honor this debt, until our specificities eventually start to resonate, from newsrooms to media schools and beyond that, in all societies willing to free themselves.

ARCHITECTURE = POWER

Stéphanie Vidal

Je ne bâtis que pierres vives ce sont des hommes. I only build with living stones, those are men. –Rabelais, French humanist (1494-1553)

The Code of Hammurabi, a basalt stone covered with cuneiform script, preserved at Le Louvre in Paris, is recognized as an important artifact for both art and history. Erected by the King of Babylon, Hammurabi, "protector of the weak and oppressed" circa 1792–1750 BC, the Code is the most complete legal compendium of Antiquity, written even before the Biblical laws. Emblematic of the Mesopotamian civilization, the stone embodied the Law into a single, indivisible object.

On rocks, monuments, or in city topologies, societies through the ages have inscribed their rules into architecture. Today, we no longer engrave laws onto stone, but architecture remains powerful at a symbolic level. ISIS, as a recent example, is destroying ancient temples in Palmyra and elsewhere in the Cradle of Humanity, because they recognize its representation of older culture. By desecrating these old monuments and broadcasting their destruction online, ISIS wants to show the world that it is destroying the memory of a period before the Prophet, and deleting the cultural symbols of Bashar Al Assad's power, making way for their new Caliphate.

Whether a smooth basalt stone, a Hindu temple, the Eiffel Tower, the pentagon, the Twin Towers, or your own house, architecture is always the manifestation of a system. A signifier of values, it contains a will to express the inherent power it represents. Building or destroying architecture is a mechanism for power to send a strong message to its audience.

Digital tools now allow further options. They can express the willingness to rebuild, and to oppose brutality with creativity; not with real stone, but with people that are the "living stones" of Rabelais.

The #NEWPALMYRA project is at the cutting-edge of this international movement. Born out of the emergency of the Syrian crisis, the #NEWPALMYRA project is an online community platform and data repository dedicated to the capture, preservation, sharing, and creative reuse of data about the ancient city of Palmyra.

In this project, the power engaged is the power of people to channel their outrage and create hope through action. Aiming to virtually reconstruct Palmyra's cultural heritage, gathering data and knowledge, #NEWPALMYRA is an expression of a collective consciousness.

People often make an opposition between the digital and the real but it is a pointless statement: the digital should be considered as an actualisation of real desire, as a space-and-time singularity where everything and everyone (even the dead and the missing) can be a presence for someone else.

We are now living in a world where the digital is omnipresent, and where power is embodied in virtual and intangible architectures, and code still comes from stone: computers are produced from geological sources such as quartz or coltan.

This so-called virtual place is made out of real materials and is based on infrastructures, such as data centers, embedded in our ecology. The Internet and all complex information systems are real architectures, and so are also an expression of power: their structure is not pre-existent, but created intentionally by their designers.

We are all evolving a world made of digital and spatial layers, where technologies are now able to follow and record our traces. The German architect Jürgen Mayer H. has expressed this contemporary double effect in his work, documenting where inhabitants leave traces of their presence over the ground and walls as they pass. According to Mayer H., "there is no such thing as a naive or innocent surface."

Archaeology is the science of identifying and studying ancient traces now preserved in ground or wall, to understand what or who left them in their present time.

In the network, we are living in the traces we leave in our everyday lives, using social media, producing or sharing content, taking pictures or being tagged by others, having a real-time narrative approach to our lives, valuing our past and accomplishments, confessing to all our followers or stalkers what we were, are, and want to be with words or metrics, and in which kind of world we wish to live.

In ancient times, the worst punishment that could ever be pronounced over someone, even worse than death, was called Damnatio Memoriae. This post-mortem sentence given to a public persona implied that their name would be erased from all public monuments, and their statues pulled down or destroyed so they would be forgotten by the people over time. But, today, we cannot be forgotten or discreet because of the constant traces we leave on the Internet.

The Internet era is the age of the Chiaroscuro, where shades of intention coexist: the impossibility of being forgotten and the craving for attention, the use of the same tool by some to preserve the history of ancient Palmyra, while others use it to delete the past and broadcast their terror and destruction; the desire, through technology, for both individual empowerment and mass surveillance.

If navigation into the digital spaces is no longer naive and can be used for surveillance, what about a system where the law could judge your intentions as well as your actions? Could we be tracked and trialed for moving freely within it?

This awful and highly complex current war is devastating Syria, harming its cultural heritage, and persecuting its "living stones." What is happening there shows the international community that people are being tracked for expressing their will for freedom, be it with something as simple as a "like" on a Facebook Page, or more arduous, such as founding an entire hackerspace.

This cruel reality has to sensitize us to the power of information technology, that it can be used, like any tool, for good or evil. The ancient Greeks were aware of the dual nature of the pharmakon: in a coercive system, the way you live or the path you take is enough to make you suspect, and those systems punish intentions and actions equally because of their potential for disruption.

The other lesson we, in the "free world" (where we don't have to be afraid of being shot by a hidden sniper), have to learn, is that liking a Facebook page, or founding a hackerspace, does not have the same cost for people living under a different system than ours. For us it's just a social interaction, for others it's a social action that can have terrible effects on their lives or the lives of their loved ones.

We have to find a way to move freely in our minds and within the systemic information architecture for it to remain a tool that can empower the people and not enable a few to reduce freedom, enact personal censorship, or jail those they perceive as threats for their oppressive systems.

Ancient Greek orators used to create mental and imaginary architecture as mnemonic techniques, to remember their long speeches so they could easily express their arguments in the Agora. Today, technology helps us acquire knowledge, express our opinions, and remind us that freedom is not something slight to be taken for granted.

We are all at risk if someone more powerful than us doesn't want us to move anymore, in the streets or on the network, so we all have to ask ourselves: What is the price we have to pay to inhabit this new architecture we are collectively building, and what do we have to do to preserve our freedom within it?

FROM OUTER SPACE

The Big Conversation Space

An Imaginary Conversation between the Author and Alex Kurtzman Regarding the Need to Base a Character in the new Star Trek Television Series (premiering on CBS Television in January 2017) on Bassel Khartabil

TBCS: Alex, thank you so much for meeting today. I know you don't have a lot of time.

AK: I don't know how you got into my office, but I´m intrigued enough to give you about 5 minutes.

TBCS: Great. Well, first of all, congratulations on being appointed executive producer of the new Star Trek series. That's a tremendous honor, and it also carries a great responsibility, a responsibility to use the show to call attention to contemporary ideas, issues, events and people that can help pave the way for a better future, a future where humanity has forged peace on Earth and can explore the universe in the quest for new knowledge and culture.

AK: Yeah, those are some of the building blocks of the Star Trek universe, sure. But we don't have the freedom to preach vague ideologies. Everything needs to be packaged in a way that will attract the most possible viewers. Do you have an idea that will help do that?

TBCS: I do have an idea, but before I get into that, I just want to remind you that no matter what impact the studios have on the decisions you make for the direction of the show, you are afforded more freedom than you may realize. You may still be somewhat enslaved to the pursuit of profit, but you can raise questions about power, you can criticize authoritarian ideologies, you can present a future that inspires people to work together now to make some semblance of it possible. You can do all of this without putting your life at risk. The studio executives might not be open to some subversive ideas, but you do not need to fear for your life, or that you could be arrested any minute for even hinting at free and open discourse.

That said, what I came here to do is tell you that there is this guy Bassel Khartabil who really needs your help, and I think you should base a character in the new Star Trek series on him. He is a wizard computer engineer, a compassionate and charismatic guy, and he has been imprisoned in Syria because of his work advocating for an open Internet. This makes for an inspiring character whose story reminds us all of the freedoms we may take for granted in our everyday life, our everyday future.

AK: Well, I do hope that we will present a future that inspires some of the audience to do something meaningful, and I am curious to hear more about this Bassel guy. But bear in mind that we have a lot of the foundational characters already set.

TBCS: You have the whole senior staff figured out?

AK: Most of them.

TBCS: Do you have an engineer? Because the Bassel character would have to be the engineer, the chief engineer. He has all the key traits of engineers throughout the series: he is a brilliant problem solver, passionate about technology, compassionate about people he works with, dedicated to making the world a better place.

AK: The chief engineers in Star Trek have been dedicated to their ships, not to making the world a better place. I mean, I'm sure they're as interested as any other graduate of Starfleet Academy who gets placed on a galaxy class starship, but that's not their focus. Their passion is the ship.

TBCS: Sure, but do we really know that? I mean, in the context of the show, the ship is their world, and they are dedicated to making that a better place, or at least a place that is not breaking down.

And besides, his dedication to helping others is precisely the quality that would make him such a valuable member of the crew. Because it's not just that he is the kind of person who could maintain the coexistent operation of a space station that is powered by the infrastructure of three different species, like Chief O´Brien in Deep Space 9, but he is also eager to share this knowledge with others and empower them through it.

AK: Hm. We have been talking about how the technology is a key gateway for audience interest, and having an engineer character who helps facilitate that knowledge and understanding is an idea worth tossing around. But, so what, these are commendable traits, sure, but what is so unique about this guy in particular that would make him a compelling character that would keep audiences riveted and interested?

TBCS: His backstory. He is a Palestinian-Syrian programmer, the son of a famous poet and a gifted engineer, who started sharing his code online for free and becoming involved in major internet projects like Mozilla and Wikipedia, He started a hackerspace in Damascus, and started Creative Commons in Syria. He vastly extended Internet access in Syria, a country with a notorious record for Internet censorship and prohibitively expensive Internet access. And his dedication to open knowledge and sharing culture made him a threat to the authoritarian government, so he was arrested.

AK: Is he still in prison?

TBCS: His whereabouts are currently unknown, he was

109

moved from his prison cell to an unknown location about a month ago, on 2 October 2015.

AK: I'm very sorry to hear that.

Well, I can tell you at least that we are interested in making some reference to the refugee crisis, at least the concept of refugees. And Internet stuff, like surveillance and censorship, are certainly hot issues today and we intend to integrate them into some storylines. But it is unlikely we will make any specific reference to Syria. This is about outer space.

TBCS: But directly referencing what is happening in Syria via this Bassel character is extremely important. Star Trek has always engaged with themes that connect to current events (relative to the time in which the series is made), and the war in Syria and its global implications is easily the most significant event occurring right now, and it's one that you have the power to impact.

AK: Again, this is a television show. Its intention is to entertain people, not to stop wars. I have about 1 minute left and am open to hearing more specifics. I am intrigued by this guy, for sure, but I would need more of a hook in order to actually consider this.

TBCS: All right. I assume you have heard of Palmyra, the ancient city in Syria that served as a vital crossroads of trade and culture for millennia until many of its archaeological wonders were senselessly destroyed by ISIS.

Well before Bassel was arrested, he was working on documenting the site via photography and 3D models, creating a virtual reconstruction that would allow people to learn more about the site and its history in an innovative, immersive fashion. He could not have known at the time that much of the actual site of Palmyra would be destroyed, indeed, at the time this prospect likely seemed impossible. But today many of the renderings he made for this project are the best surviving sources of data about the site.

AK: That's incredible. Are these renderings or this data publicly available?

TBCS: Yes, and they are in the public domain. There is a movement, a community and a web site called New Palmyra where artists, scientists, and designers are coming together to share, explore, and build upon Bassel´s data and renderings, to virtually reconstruct Palmyra's heritage and in so doing build cultural understanding that transcends geographic and political borders.

AK: That sounds pretty well in line with Star Trek´s mission, and like something that could make for a great holodeck program. And since the files are in the public domain already, we would have significantly more freedom to experiment than we would if we had to construct them from scratch.

Well, I think it's been more than 5 minutes. I have enjoyed this conversation and I will see what I can do. At the very least, I think we can name a shuttle or an exoplanet after New Palmyra.

TBCS: So long as there is a Bassel riding in that shuttle.

FREE SOFTWARE ECONOMICS

hellekin, Jaromil, radium, and Christian Grothoff

Fifteen years ago, in his seminal article Code Is Law, Lawrence Lessig identified a problematic: *"The most important contexts of regulation in the future will affect Internet commerce: where the architecture does not enable secure transactions."* Today, European free software researchers are implementing innovative solutions to address this and other issues that will shape digital economics in the near future.

We argue that beyond regulation, code embeds politics. We'll introduce two projects we think will transform not only how we conduct economic transactions online, but which also hold the potential to radically change the global balance of economic power.

Freecoin is a social digital currency based on the blockchain technology of Bitcoin but which relies on a "social proof of work" instead of the original brute-force algorithmic proof of work used in Bitcoin. Freecoin was developed by the Dyne Foundation, a free culture foundry based in the Netherlands, and now a European Research Network. Freecoin is Project no. 610349 in the FP7 – CAPS framework, under the Decentralised Citizens ENgagement Technologies (D-CENT) project.

GNU Taler is the Taxable Anonymous Libre Economic Reserve, a new electronic payment system under development at Inria, the French National Institute for Information and Automation Research, and the Technical University of Munich (TUM). It aims at delivering an online and offline payment solution for various established currencies such as Euro, U.S. Dollar, or even electronic currencies such as Freecoin.

Together they implement a unique electronic solution for mainstream economics beyond payment. They were specifically designed with social values addressing the shortcomings of both early electronic currencies such as Bitcoin, enabling a variety of local currencies to work together, extending transactions to non-monetary domains such as distributed storage, and drastically limiting the criminal use of money. Their combined approaches unfold a many-to-many platform suitable for daily use from global micro-payments to local social currencies.

Bitcoin was the first digital currency to appear on the Internet. It implements a distributed and authenticated public ledger called the blockchain, whose mode of operation is based on decentralized consensus. The blockchain replaces the bank: it uses cryptographic techniques to regulate the emission of coins and verify transactions between peers.

The design of Bitcoin has definitive shortcomings: first of all it's very volatile. By the time this article was finished, its value was down to USD 402.7 after reaching USD 479 earlier during the day. As all finalized Bitcoin transactions appear in the blockchain, the whole market is transparent, and a coin's history can be used to connect identities to addresses. To avoid double spending, no bitcoin transaction can be reversed, which means the buyer is not protected against fraud from the seller, nor addressing errors. By design, Bitcoin rewards early adopters. Finally, the proof of work requires a significant amount of computing power which translates into high energy costs.

FREECOIN

Freecoin is a set of tools that let people run a reward scheme that is transparent and auditable by other organizations.

Designed for participatory and democratic organizations willing to incentivize participation it is, unlike centralized banking databases, a social currency that is reliable, simple, and
resilient. Technical and design elements shape a way to le-
gitimize the bottom-up process using audit of cryptographic
blockchain technologies such as decentralized storage, ubiquitous wallets, and ad-hoc social remuneration systems.

The Freecoin project insists on the need to strengthen
the democratic debate necessary to consolidate and preserve
the management of economic transactions, especially those
with a social orientation, inside the local monetary circuit.
It focuses on complementary currency design to allocate and
distribute credit created among engaged members, using a
reputation as risk management system.

Citizens can collectively define their social needs using a
participatory deliberation based on "social sustainability":
without participation, local monetary circuits run the risk
to remain too little, too dependent on the local political cycles, too far from the real demand that may be expressed
by the local economic system. Choices need to be informed
with social objectives and ethical criteria to properly allocate resources and investments.

The Freecoin / D-CENT project is an experiment in digital social currency design that aims at solving two problems: (1) the vulnerability of centralized information systems, whose integrity can be jeopardized by compromising
a few points of failure, and (2) the management of digitally
distributed trust to make sure that different organizations
which may not share trust can agree and verify the integrity
of a transaction history, even in the absence of the other organization.

1) *Complementary currency governance systems*: with a
minimalistic reinterpretation of the blockchain technology,
the Freecoin Toolchain is a toolkit for community members

to easily access and decide on the features of their currency system by using a decentralized governance structure – essentially, bringing back human intervention to oppose the high-frequency trading algorithms (Durbin, 2010). A system for collective deliberation on the decisions regarding digital currency will allow users to engage in collective monetary policy-making.

2) *Distributed trust management systems*: reputation is the basis for trust and decision-making. Putting together trust and the blockchain, the Freecoin Toolchain allows for the design and prototyping of systems aimed at managing social currency in a community, i.e. reputation in a decentralized fashion. The use of micro-endorsements allows the even spreading of risk among participants, and the rewarding of the best political contributions (similar to the participatory budgeting in Iceland). In a municipality, the use of those credits as loyalty scheme vouchers lowers the risk to promote proposals that go against the common interest of the citizenry.

The issuance of new coins is a technology-driven mechanism based on a consensus algorithm that neutralizes counterfeiting. However, this may also be seen as a departure from an active and critical engagement among humans and machines, whereby the creation of money in the system is motivated by social interactions for the common good, rather than by exclusively hashing cycles and shortsighted money-making. Therefore, the task of the Freecoin / D-CENT research is to redefine Bitcoin's 'proof of work' and the reward of a blockchain system, to devolve power into the hands of people through a democratic decision process. The outcome of this shift in design is twofold: (1) people engage in transactions that have real world desirable impact that they produce and collectively construct; (2) new participants can enjoy an egalitarian economic environment by avoiding the undesirable condition of structural advantage by early adopters of a currency. At the same time, this allows complete democratic oversight of transaction history and collective deliberation on social currency system rules of engagement and reward.

The Freecoin project is licensed as Affero GNU General Public License version 3 or later to make sure that all uses, commercial or non-commercial, will provide access to the source code, be it modified or not.

GNU TALER

At IETF 93, Edward Snowden said via videoconference: *"I think one of the big things that we need to do, is we need to get away from true-name payments on the Internet. The credit card payment system is one of the worst things that happened for the user, in terms of being able to divorce their access from their identity."* So while obviously some people do not care much about their privacy, we do think that many will heed his words once a viable alternative exists. Identity theft, fraud, convenience and efficiency gains are other reasons why consumers or merchants are likely to be excited about adopting Taler.

While our initial market is likely to be technological enthusiasts with a focus on privacy, we believe that the technology is applicable in general for all payments (in online stores and physical stores) assuming sufficient engineering effort (integration, ease of use, etc.) is put behind it.

However, as the receivers of funds are not anonymous and can be audited and taxed by the state, Taler's market does not include tax evasion, money laundering, human trafficking and any other forms of illegal trade that have ballooned the popularity of Bitcoin.

Established payment systems, such as the ubiquitous

credit cards, try to authenticate the user making the payment. In contrast, Taler uses cryptography to secure the value and validity of the payment. As a result, identity theft is no longer a problem for customers using Taler, and merchants also do not have to worry about the theft of sensitive customer information. Naturally, customers may reveal their identity (i.e. for shipping), but they are not forced to by the payment system. In contrast to previous research designs, Taler provides stronger assurances for the customer's privacy (including better than BitCoin, where transactions are linkable). We are also the first electronic payment system of this type that supports giving change (i.e. pay 5 EUR with a 100 EUR coin and get 95 EUR in electronic change) with these privacy assurances. Taler can even provide refunds to customers without violating their anonymity. At the same time, transaction costs are several orders of magnitude cheaper than those with BitCoin-technologies. At scale, we expect transaction costs to be lower than those for existing credit cards, as expenses from fraud by consumers, merchants or identity theft are prevented by the cryptographic protocol.

Unlike BitCoin, Taler does not introduce a new currency but merely provides digital representations of existing currencies (such as EUR, USD or even BTC), eliminating the risk from currency fluctuations introduced by payment systems that introduce a new currency, such as BitCoin, Alt-Coins, or Stellar.

Our system consists of various components operated by different groups. The mint creating the digital coins is mostly finished and just undergoing additional testing and audits. The mint is also the most complex part of the design. Even after this is finished, we still need to integrate the mint with the banking system of each respective country to perform wire transfers. This is a one-time expense per banking system. For the customers, we need to ensure that the "wallet" application works well for their respective platform. Our initial implementation is for Firefox, ports to other browsers and native apps for mobile phones will require more work. The wallet is simpler than the mint, but still non-trivial especially if we want to make it easy to use and nice to look at.

Finally, each merchant will require some modifications to their business logic to integrate the new payment system. While these modifications are way smaller and easier than the mint or the wallet, there are of course many more businesses platforms than browsers or banking systems. Hence, while the work for an individual store should be tiny, this will be a major effort. We are trying to document our protocol and prototypes and will provide reference implementations in various languages to facilitate this integration.

GNU Taler is free software released under the terms of the GNU General Public License version 3 or later.

BEYOND CAPITALISM

hellekin

The future was to be excellent. Thanks to the endless progress of human knowledge, technology would deliver the right solution at the right time. As industrial powers scaled up, though, and hacked their way out of diminishing returns with brute force, the picture of a bright future turned out to be as naive and grotesque as the vision of the year 2000 as seen from 1902.

Modernity is totalitarian. Following Descartes' proclamation of the prevalence of the mind over matter, modern science engaged in a process of stripping away uncertainty and contradiction. The world of the mechanical clock was thoroughly explained, controlled, and made to serve mankind, in accordance with the Biblical injunction of breeding and multiplying, and using the God-given resources of the Earth. But the world is not complicated: it's complex, and contradiction is built-in.

Capitalism was a fantastic booster that propelled us from candle light to LED, from parchment to digital computer, from horse carriage to spacecraft. Its premises, though, require endless growth, and some time would pass before we could replicate our own spaceship Earth. As it attained global operational scale, capitalism was panting like a hamster on its wheel ready for a heart attack. The myth of progress was on artificial respiration. The capitalist system now reached capacity and still requires new markets, better outcomes, more efficient ways to suck fossil and mineral resources off the ground. The system is ticking seamlessly: grab a piece of primary rainforest, cut down the trees for construction and furniture, plant soy to feed millions of pigs on thousands of farms, then when the soil is sucked dead 5 years later, mine for minerals and frack for oil shale.

We would already need to harvest the resources of four planets like Earth to keep up with the pace at which the global industrial war machine exploits and decays our environment. But we barely can send robots to Mars, so this option is off. We could wait for the next super-technology-that-will-save-us-all, but as Jevons observed, any technological progress increases the efficiency of resource use, consumption of resources rise as more demand is met. If a new engine can be made more cheaply, it will sell more, and the net result will be a faster and stronger pressure on resources. Even if such super-technology could potentially appear, it remains a big IF, and would it come in time for us to reverse the damage already done to the fragile conditions that maintain the Earth livable for our species?

An obvious course of action would be to stop running and relinquish a bit of comfort to bring about the possibility of our survival. This solution, though, requires the end of growth, which fundamentally contradicts the extraction system that fueled the technological boom in the last two centuries. Given the importance, in terms of scale, of the problem at hand, the possibility of a peaceful solution remains both remote and indispensable. Other paths can only amplify the crisis and lead to catastrophe.

Thought, here, has reached its limits: only action remains possible. Mindful, ethical, and compassionate action. Loving, caring, and sensible action may unlock the true potential of a successful humanity, and freedom, yet undefined, remains a golden key.

AFFORDANCES

QUEERING

Natacha Roussel

From 23 to 24 May, femhack organized an international hackathon in the loving memory of Sabeen Mahmud, getting together amongst a large number of feminist hackerspaces locally and around the world.

Sabeen Mahmud was a Pakistani activist fighting for human rights in Pakistan. She was the co-founder and director of the second floor (T2F), a cafe in Karachi. She also had been the president of Karachi's branch of deTiE (The Indus Entrepreneurs), a not-for-profit organisation dedicated to promoting entrepreneurial spirit. On 24 April 2014, she was shot down by unidentified gunmen while coming back from the seminar she had just hosted at T2F, examining issues and triggering awareness about people who had disappeared in Baluchistan, a province of northern Pakistan.

A year after her death, we had the desire to express our solidarity online and off-line, as a network of feminist spaces for resistance, being transnationals and postcolonialists. Furthermore, this event allowed us to more clearly define our network of solidarity. We do have a shared discourse, and we also work to appropriate technological space to the benefit of our communities. We feel we are engaged in a larger process that fundamentally nurtures our small community-based structures. Most of us consider we are in a sphere of action that overcomes the deconstruction process needed to get out of a proprietary way of life. We put forward alternative ways of life and solidarity networks. Our next concern is to secure our existing structures: this is not an easy process, as fragility is also a definitive asset allowing for sensitivity and understanding. However, while numerous, our structures lack the sufficient visibility that would allow better protection, and consequently it keeps being difficult to identify everyone.

This day was the occasion of an encounter that has enabled us to identify one another better: since then; we continue to exchange messages on a dedicated mailing list that helps us to know each other better. However, it still is very difficult to completely identify each other in the varied materiality of our different commitments. Since that day, the more than 30 structures in which we are participating have developed a series of approaches to the issues, going from Wikipedia editathons to augment feminist content on Wikipedia, to Women in Surveillance meetups, citizen-sensing endeavors, or small exchange and programming groups. However, despite the persistent relations that we are creating and the commonality of our interests and attitudes, it remains a complex challenge to understand and assess the personality of each of us in an always-transient state of being, as people are involved in projects with different levels of risks.

All continents were represented during that event, but the most numerous were situated in Latin America, maybe because of the beauty of a language practice that has invented a written transgender form; for example: "somos guapxs" is the transgender form of "we are beautiful."

NOMADIC FAMILY

Natacha Roussel

The problem of the costs within the schizoid logic of our times concerns mostly potestas, the quantitative, not potentia, or incorporeal intensities. –Rosi Braidotti, Nomadic Theory

The question of costs often translates into issues of scale and scalability that are dominant in technological societies. The "scale solutionism" starts from the desire to solve cost problems and ends in hyper-control, restriction, dissociation and finally disaster conducted by non-aware necropolitics, where the politics of death systematically takes over the politics of life (Mbembe 2003), increasing the costs of freedom. In such instances, when the state of power constantly refers to a state of exception in order to overcome the rule of preservation and the social limit, Achille Mbembe explains that it seems figures of sovereignty develop a general concern that is not the preservation of the commons and liveliness, but the spreading of death and the material destruction of bodies and populations: Bassel Khartabil is, unfortunately, a direct victim.

In this context, it is impossible to address the problem of costs without transforming our relation to the existing system. Always confronted with an impossible dilemma of sustainability, we need to envision different ways to face this situation. While costs are most often evaluated as a quantifiable asset, this quantification is mainly calculated in regards to an actual neo-liberal vision of individual self and proprietary systems. It seems crucial to envision different avenues to overcome the cost issues, and define new criteria of cost evaluation that could lead to re-thinking the free production processes in a different organization scheme, resulting in the main question: we should ask ourselves if the costs of freedom cannot be addressed as a qualitative process rather than a quantitative one.

Practically, to enforce such a process, only the diversity of networks can help secure our individual endeavors; therefore, the re-evaluation of the cost of freedom should start from the premises of community and collective approaches to production and network realization, which support non-proprietary production and distribution of information. Resulting from the contestation of the need to encompass our work in active F/LOSS and open source developments, is the necessity to situate our social connection and embodiment leading to new contexts for such a production. Starting from an assertion of the actual situation, we are looking at ways to think complexly with regards to freedom issues, and explore how to co-synchronise so that the relation that feeds our networks can exist despite actual power issues.

A Foucauldian view of the actual context would present, coextensively to the rise of power structures, the formulation of scientific discourse as the cause of actual costly body politics. While modernity has attached its project to a rational view of the world based on a clear mind-body split that is exponentially growing along with technological development, this disunion nurtures the dissociative powers of capitalism. Despite all efforts to enforce a discourse promoting technology as a substitute for human relation, it is, however, certain that the posthuman does not map to the network, and more specifically it appears that the proposed agenda of dematerialisation and autonomous artificial intelligent networks is a fantasmagorical construction (Hayles 2001). Therefore, it is from a holistic perspective that the observation of the actual complexity needs to be undertaken. In the context of a huge up-scaling of human presence on earth and the growth of social control apparatus, can an examination of relational complexity bring us towards social sustainability, and what would be the sensitive approach that could ground an exchange system, and lead it towards a sustainable expansion?

A holistic setup would allow us to spare ourselves by leaving the costs for freedom at the expense of the potestas while reacting in diverse and unstructured networks, and at a molecular level to reach full potentia. We are looking for ways to confront necropolitics and trigger liveliness; in this context liveliness is to be thought as a spiritual process that further constitutes the grounds for a different politics. Indeed, a different approach to politics needs to be rooted in the life of the spirit that is not afraid of death, and instead of looking for substitutes and technological prosthesis, it fully assumes death as a constituent of human relation and organisation while it looks beyond the unitary vision of the self, to molecular transformations as a way to synchronize to the world in a deeply transformative process (Braidotti 2011).

In response to this statement, several issues need to be addressed that would further ground the development of our community processes, based on a long history and knowledge of existing knowledge. Some affordances might lead to explore different relational setups that would help to transpose the question of costs.

TRANSMISSION: While power relations build over cycles of crisis, they seem to destroy reference points and instrumentalize history to the service of immediate power relations. Indeed, it is clear that technological breakthroughs importantly transform relational processes, but contrary to what we once have thought, they do not expose the processes of power. On another hand, critical discourses, tools and concepts are developed through time, and they often are sourced from fragile social structures, either isolated individuals or community structures. As a consequence of this fragility, they most often repeatedly deal with recurrent issues, while transmission lines are broken, they each time face the need to develop a discourse and solutions. It is important to intervene at community scale in the process of transmission to create community genealogies and a history of community movement through time. This would allow us to keep those principles active during technological transitions. One of the possibilities is to expose current technological communities to existing social science and allow for transdisciplinarity and politicization of the discourse. The project of hackerspaces workshops, for example, inscribes itself into a transactional process of transmission through a collective community context.

BIOPOWER: As it appears that sovereignty stands as a condition of control, the question of the unicity of self, is again a transient issue persisting across time and through technologies. Variations of intensity characterize the thinking subject and are mostly characterized at its boundaries; those variations set a relational process independent from the view of a holistic body. They in principle go far further than the limits of human species in setting the potential of transformation into a process of becoming. According to Rosi Braidotti, this denaturalization process is one of the effects of technological progress in fields such as biogenetics where we integrate different species in an inter-evolutionary process.

TRANSFORMATION: After a consciousness-rising process triggered by the awareness of a state of dismay, it could be timely to consider, observe and acknowledge a trans-species potential for knowledge diversity leading to social sustainability. This process can be thought as both individual and collective, implying both personal mutation, and through collective support, a larger transformational process. Being in the instant and acting from this perspective, and responding to the trigger of the momentum is a way to reach the acknowledgment of the possibility of instantaneous transformation. Variations of codes, genres and modalities of expression of the idea see transposition as a possible solution for genetic transmutation and exchange.

SELF-SUFFICIENCY

Pauline Gadea

I decided 2 years ago to leave jobs in the media to go learning how to make cheese. I saw this as a step towards essential freedom.

Beyond choosing a life much more in touch with nature and craft, it would give me the freedom to carry around with me the ability to eventually fit with a concrete valuable knowledge into communities that aim at producing their own means of subsistence as much as possible, maybe creating my own means of subsistence in the end. It represented a step which would make it possible for me to build a life outside both the mainstream work system and the food system. I see both of those systems as freedom down-takers. My statement was more or less "I want to create something I would be proud of with my bare hands in a settled place, which would help to tend to freedom for me and a small community I choose. If not, I feel like I m neutral in the best case scenario in a path to global freedom, feeding a mass system which deprives it in the worst way of looking at it."

This vision, of freedom linked with self-sufficiency in food supplies and self-determination in terms of human organisation, is commonly shared, at least as an ideal goal, but is also seen as quite extreme in terms of the changes it requires for most people's ways of living. Making a step towards it was a way to challenge my own motivation, my own limits in relation to this fantasized ideal of real, deep, freedom and its connection with a rural life.

In order to learn properly, I had to deal amongst other things with the traditional farming work culture as an employee, a reality which was further from the concept of freedom than I had experienced in all other work situations, in terms of hierarchy, of hour-based deadline pressure, of physical commitment. I didn't fit in but I still had to learn, and earning money in the process also was quite essential.

You see your friends obtaining more freedom and self-realisations by more classical means. Mainly by just mastering their work field little by little, you see them having little by little better salaries, wider responsibilities, recognition and range of action in what they are doing. Then you start to wonder why you have to make it so complicated... I questioned my choices. Of course, making cheese does not provide the same kind of freedom I was after when I decided on this change of life, but it still gives the comfort and confidence I might need for any future achievement.

In the end, setting a precise, high goal of freedom as a core preoccupation in my life as a starting point hasn't led me to more actual freedom (yet), but it obliges me to ask myself very often what is that I'm doing and why am I doing it. Answering those questions makes the commitment deeper and slowly creates the connections I need to live a life closer to my ideals, like a vow I made that forces me to be brave when I feel insecure about what I am doing, and making it silly to worry about where I am going to keep those three pieces of furniture for a while.

COLLECTIVE VALIDATION

ginger coons

A friend of mine—a multimedia artist and a community organizer—once referred to taking a job at a commercial software company as "becoming a civilian," as something that might be a little more relaxing, a little lower pressure than what she was used to. What she meant was that by just taking a job, a normal job, with normal expectations, she was opting to get out of the public eye for a while, to stop doing work that could be seen, judged, and assessed by the whole world.

I know the feeling. In all of the free cultural work I've done over the last six years, one of my most pervasive anxieties has been the feeling that I work in public, that everyone is always looking over my shoulder—or could be if they wanted to. It's a difficult feeling to come to terms with, even if it's based on one of the most potent and valuable principles of free culture: transparency.

For the last five years, I've worked on a project called Libre Graphics magazine. The point of it—the whole point, to my mind—is to show off just how good graphic design and art done with Free/Libre and Open Source software, standards, licenses, and methods can be. It's the whole package, and the whole package includes a kind of extreme transparency. For five years, my collaborators and I have stuck all of our working files into a public version control system. For five years, we've opened ourselves up to scrutiny and criticism not just when we put out an issue, but before, during our development process. As with free software, one of our goals has been to release early and often, to make our work public so it can become better. We don't hide our production files and then release when they're perfect. It's nerve wracking to work in public like that, even if most

131

people aren't digging through the git repository and looking at our working files.

It's nerve wracking and sometimes even scary to open yourself up to the potential for scrutiny all the time. But it's still valuable. If the point of Libre Graphics magazine has been to show that F/LOSS and free cultural principles apply outside of software, then that potential for scrutiny has been essential. If the point is to show that designers can do high-quality work with F/LOSS, then the potential for scrutiny is also the opportunity for someone who's feeling uncertain about even trying something new to come along and see how we did it. The publicness is a chance for others to follow in our footsteps and to use our mistakes to do things better in the future, or to skip over some of the tough bits. That publicness, in short, is worth something.

But on a personal level, it's still nerve wracking. It can be frustrating to pour your heart—and worse, your time and your effort—into work that's totally voluntary, with almost all rewards intrinsic. The freedom to create, to put something out, to experiment, to try, is also the freedom to be ignored, to be undervalued, and at worst, to be bashed or harassed for your efforts. You can't rely on the positive feedback from others to keep you going. You have to enjoy and value what you're doing for itself. And if you succeed, if what you make is something that others find valuable, that breeds the expectation that you'll continue, even if the odds get long. It can feel as if you've gone from being ignored to being taken for granted.

And then there's the old aphorism about free software being free like speech, not like beer—free as in freedom, not as in money. But the best variation I've seen is free like a puppy: if you adopt it, you become responsible for it. You care for it. By taking up the chance to do something, you take up the responsibility to keep doing it, often at personal expense. And it can get pretty expensive. It can be expensive in the normal ways, what we typically mean when we use the word "expense," but more importantly, it can become emotionally expensive.

Celebrities and politicians get paid commensurate with the expectation that their work will be judged by the public. People working with F/LOSS and free culture generally don't. We do it because we love it, or at the very least, because we believe in it. And we believe in currencies other than money, too. We often believe that the work is its own pay and that it doesn't take money to be worth the occasional frustration of having others be demanding of our time and effort. But the costs are real.

One of the other costs of freedom—of the transparency I value so highly in free culture—is feeling as if you're never allowed to get something right. When your work is done in public and when its success is often a matter of public opinion, it's easy to feel as if every decision you make has the potential to be second-guessed. For every little snippet of positive feedback, for every bit of evidence you get that your work has made a difference, there's a horde of people who are happy to tell you every little thing you've done wrong. That happens when you work in public, and it can be powerfully demoralizing.

Because it's worse for ongoing projects, it can make you wish you hadn't chosen to aim for continuity and accountability. A one-off, something you make because you feel like it, throw out into the world, and then don't plan to invest in over the long-term, doesn't need the ongoing commitment, the continued desire to engage. When you explicitly choose to do something in the long term, to commit to a project that lasts and grows, when you commit to becoming a fixture, the drip-erosion that comes from the second-guessing can be enough to scour away the desire that originally drove the project.

When we build free cultural projects, we try to enrich the world. We do things, not just for our own benefit, but because we think we can do something good for others. Releasing work under licenses that allow others to reproduce, to rethink, to remake and to re-release is an explicit commitment to the commons, and to the idea that we can build on the work of others, and that others can improve or change our work. When we undertake to do work in public, we commit to something similar. We commit to the idea that others can derive value from seeing our process and that we can grow and improve from having our process intervened in and commented upon. When we build collaborative projects, we make a commitment to inclusion, to allowing others to work with us if they share an interest in the project and willingness to contribute. These are valuable commitments, driven by a desire to help others and to enrich the commons. They're important and they matter. These commitments are the foundation of free software and free culture.

Principles are important. Ideals are important. Sometimes, though, it feels as if we get crushed under the weight of their downsides. It can be profoundly demoralizing when it feels as if most of the feedback you get is negative. And that doesn't need to happen. I long for the day when we all—even as strangers who only meet when judging each others' work—think about how much effort, time and personal expense goes into the things we release. I long for the day when we decide that looking after other creators and contributors matters, even if we don't really know each other. I long for the day when there's more positive affirmation than judgement. And most of all, I long for the day when we recognize that we're all mostly fighting for the same thing—for meaningful contributions to the commons, for a way to build culture together. I so look forward to the day when we can accept not just that others produce work we can judge, but that the people producing those works are humans, as fallible and delicate as we are, and that they deserve not just our feedback, but our praise and encouragement.

TRANSDISCIPLINARITY

Mélanie Dulong de Rosnay

I fell under the spell of sharism in 2003 when I started the Creative Commons France chapter with the full support of my then Ph.D. advisor and the director of our research center. Since then, my participation in the movement has landed me a blissful life with lifelong friends, love, and several paid jobs and grants both in my country and abroad with lovely, smart, dedicated and gifted people animated by the values of open access, open science, open licensing, peer production, the public domain and the commons.

In 2007, several teams coordinated by Creative Commons Italy received a grant from the European Commission to start Communia network in the public domain and support our work. All this provided opportunities to have a political impact and travel. It is possible to develop serious research and policy contributions with a network of amazing colleagues all over the world, people coming from diverse backgrounds who share similar ideals.

The cruel detention of Bassel Khartabil reminds us of the incredible luck of living in such a privileged environment with freedom of expression. My only social cost has been exclusion by conservative people from whom I needed neither approval nor friendship, and this doesn't even happen so much anymore since openness is becoming more politically correct and even hyped in Western culture.

To newcomers wondering if the cost in terms of time and efforts is worth the involvement: it is nothing compared to the inspiration gained and the joy and pride of contributing to a global movement that is developing positive alternatives to enclosures, and promoting social justice, freedom and access to knowledge, information, culture and education, good food and medicine.

Even though some of us are techno-idealist, our work is not, neither is it economically insane, but rather highly political and ideological. Freedom of knowledge and circulation are battles to win over the corruption and censorship of those whose addiction to unlimited commodification, unsustainable growth and a vision of development based on globalized extractivism that prevents personal and collective development and the right to a good life for 99% of the population.

RESILIENT NETWORKS

Jean-Noel Montagné

Makers

In France, most of the Makers are hobbyists, technolovers, geeks that create for fun, for local glory and some, for business. But few of them are makers for social or political goals. Most of the objects created in fablabs and makerspaces in the last years are useless regarding the urgent problems of the planet. Because the planet is on fire. Climate crisis. Energy crisis. Demography crisis. Water crisis. Metals crisis. Financial crisis. Education crisis, even crisis of mental health because of the abuse of digital communication.

But stop ! it's enough ! Come back to transformaking, No-one wants to hear about this crude reality !

Resilient Society

And that's the problem: historians studying the extinction of old civilisations in the last millennia have discovered that leaders and populations knew about the perfectly serious problems of their time, but they ignored the scientific advice and all indicators turning to red, until the end. We are doing exactly the same and we don't have a lot of time to act. We must transform all sectors of the society before the conjunction of some important crisis, and transformakers will help us to do it.

In the global village, industry is totally dependent on flux, networks of raw materials, energy, goods, tools, components, distribution and transportation. Any failure in one spot can disturb or stop the whole chain, from extraction of raw materials to distribution of goods. This interdependency is an enormous fragility in the context of the coming crisis, and transformakers can help us to break it.

138

We have all noticed that we can't really count on our political systems to find efficient solutions. We know we can only count on ourselves. We, citizens, can build resilient communities, based on small structures, driven by direct democracy, and based on big citizenship networking. We have the digital tools and the network to do it.

Transformakers have a key role in this transition from globalisation to resilience.

Global Crisis

The COP21 UN conference about climate change offers to limit the rise of the global temperature to two degrees more. Accepting 2 degrees more, on average, for the planet, however, is accepting violent transformations of the climate that will create a giant loss of biodiversity, massive extinction of species in earth and ocean during those years. Two degrees more will also create huge environmental and social disorders, instability everywhere, wars, starvation. Hundreds of millions of refugees will have to move, dismantling completely the actual geopolitic equilibrium.

Pure water is also missing everywhere because of very bad management, but the most important resource crisis will come with metals and oil. We live now with the illusion of infinite resources, but this new prosperity will have an end. The planet has a limited quantity of fossil energy in the ground, and we are reaching the limits in one or two generations, in our children's lifetimes. No lessons have been taken from the 2008 crash. Improvements in high-frequency trading do not actually cover the many debts of countries and their people. Big monetary regulators are also provoking also a crisis of democracy, of citizenship, of trust in each other.

A new era of chaos brings an opportunity for radically changing the system in good directions.

Transformaking

How can transformakers help in the context of global crisis ?

By helping us to change the scale from globalization to small resilient networked communities, to rebuild real direct democracy and redefine urbanisation and the usage of our lands. By helping us to rebuild our social organisation around knowledge networks. By helping us to harvest clean energy, renewable energy everywhere, and to share it. By helping us to redefine our material strategies, our industrial strategies. By creating new models for currencies and money circulation.

We discover today that good social, environmental and financial practices have always existed. Transformaking is the common behaviour in many communities in the world, especially in rural areas: do it yourself, DIWithOthers, Do It Together: people invent tools and technologies adapted to their context, to their pragmatic needs, using few resources, using local resources. People repair, they recycle, they hack objects, they transmit the knowledge to young generations. Poor countries will not suffer as much as rich countries in the chaotic future, because they have always lived in the Transformaking way.

In social organisation, all over the world, small communities use solidarity structures, monetary arrangements, like barter systems that can be considered as local money, in a pure peer-to-peer exchange. The organisation of traditional communities offers big lessons for us and this model just needs digital tools to be adapted to small communities in the modern world.

Sharing knowledge = open sourcing

Transformaking officially arrived in our society 30 years ago, when hackers started to change the world with the first open source software licences, one of the most powerful political acts of the XXth century. Artists followed the movement 20 years ago with open source documents and artwork licences, and some makers have taken another important step, ten years ago, with Open Source Hardware licences. This is transformaking: changing the society by offering alternatives containing the values of solidarity and knowledge.

Open source technologies, from their concept of production and distribution, open the possibility of a total citizen control on technology. It's now possible to envision human-scale industry, citizen industry, decentralized industry, like our ancestors did before the Industrial Revolution. The ecosystem of transformaking is self-organised around knowledge networks. Any technological process can be created or improved by transformakers, because networks of knowledge, networks of citizen research, networks of materials and networks of components exists underground. In the recent years, transformakers have started to design and build very complicated open source machines related to many sectors of industry, and citizen research now attacks topics such as high tech medicine, nuclear physics, nanotechnologies or genetics. All in Open Source: Free Libre Open Source Software (FLOSS) and Free Libre Open Source Hardware (FLOSH).

Patents are living their last twenty years, even in some very protected niche industries, such as medical equipment: look at their websites and initiatives.

One could argue that hackers, transformakers are not regulated by authorities, certifications, ethics commitees and could launch projects which are dangerous projects for society. But no. They wouldn't. Because transformakers are a network of citizens, we are self-organized and the debate is always open in open source technologies. Creation and correction of code, of designs, follows real democratic rules, much less dangerous than government or military-security projects. How to promote more transformaking in society?

First by protecting the Internet and net neutrality. Networking tools are essential for democracy and sharing of knowledge. Big companies like Facebook and GAFAM are silently killing the Internet by replacing all software on the client side, by services driven by their data-sucker servers, associated to the Panopticon of the Internet Of Things. New global totalitarianism.

We can promote transformaking

- by supporting hackers and transformaker projects through crowdfunding
- by opening new medialabs, hackerspaces, makerspaces, and open laboratories, and specializing in them (biology, health, agriculture, etc)
- by opening places in cities to dismantle, repair, recycle objects, parts, etc
- by choosing to use open source software and open source hardware when available
- by funding P2P and common goods initiatives in all sectors of society
- by installing education programmes about hacking, about transformaking
- by choosing slow and resilient communication technologies for establishing strong communication and education networks.

Post capitalist era

Transition from globalisation to new resilient small-scale networked societies is necessary and must start now. Transformakers are the first explorers of the post-capitalist era. But they don't move alone. Many new citizen organisations, new-style political movements are following the movement, but most of them ignore what transformakers are doing.

Transformakers have started to transform the society through new behaviours based on local resources, local solidarities, self-management and direct democracy, and based on global communication and global exchange of knowledge.

Instead of losing energy to promote this vision into standard political systems, we need to start building initiatives around us, responding to our values, co-existing with the actual system, and if our alternatives are good, if our models take sense into the society, they will naturally replace the old system, without war, without revolutions.

Let's do it. DIY, DIT, DIWO, DIN[17]

---

[17]Do-It-Yourself, Do-It-Together, Do-It-With-Others, Do-It-Now

RECONCILIATION

hellekin, Natacha Roussel, and Pauline Gadea

Like a teenager discovering the shortcomings of the father, 21st Century humans want to break free from a paternalist system that cannot address complexity. They start looking after each other and invent new associative institutions for solidarity, and take the responsibility for their own future without waiting for the next false promise to come true. In the dying liberal system, the promise of personal growth and individual freedom is considered the key to a successful life and-or entrepreneurship. In this context, however, individual freedom is often understood as the capacity to do anything you like without responsibility. In the upcoming social re-organization, stability is grounded on free, voluntary association, and a new concept of freedom is necessary to keep the system from running out of control. We must acknowledge that with freedom comes responsibility. If "with power comes great responsibility", political power brings the most responsibility, therefore it must respect individual freedom in the first place.

The antagonistic contradiction between global and individual freedoms brings on the notion of choice and responsibility to create the balance and resolve it at another level of reality. Gaining power is not anymore a question of taking it, but to accept responsibility at a global scale. Not only to accumulate knowledge but to learn to be human, and learn to live together. The pathway to a different socio-political organization starts with the deconstruction of the fundamentals of our civilization: individual freedom is most interesting in all aspects when it is measured with regard to the social constraints, it then becomes productive of worthy social and collective outcomes. Each individual can then root her personal development both in a local and global community, therefore reflecting personal action to nurture both the personal and the collective. Interdependence enabling self-determination can activate personal freedom as a responsible asset. A severe impeachment to self-determination is paternalism, a principal regulator of our infantilizing civilization. It can be retraced up and until liberalism and must disappear from a different organizational model if we are to achieve global individual and responsible freedom, responding to the injunction to "think global, act local".

Free culture is all about addressing this contradiction as it emerges from this polarized tension. It produces the actual means and technical tools both inspired by those issues and created to resolve them. But free culture was born in reaction to the impeachment of self-determination and it struggles to blossom beyond resentment. As it rejects the paternalism of established institutions, it is harder for free culture organizations to benefit from the synergies of interdependence that could enable it to become a tangible way out of dying social structures. It rises the essential question of scale of organisazion, on which contributions here above express diverging opinions.

A recurrent pattern in free culture and free software is the lack of means to achieve stated goals, that ends up limiting the scope of action. Proponents of scaling up to big entities, as well as proponents of small, resistant networks need to overcome their differences: both approaches present opportunities and caveats, both are complementary. Large entities have easier access to capital, and can unfold economies of scale, as long as their action is focused and directed. But that comes at the price of slowness and a lack of resilience. On the contrary, distributed networks must offset the costs of their autonomy and their speed in line with a lack of funding that can be paralyzing.

Large entities are more likely to obtain public grants, as they can invest in the time and skills required to write acceptable applications. It involves technical and administrative knowledge and know-how that is often lacking in existing solidarity networks. But such grants generally allocate funds to tightly focused projects, serving specialized tasks and positions. Meanwhile small networks are often divergent, exploratory, involving multiple skills from a variety of disciplines: this work cannot be covered by grants which impose accountable production plans.

The question of how to enable complementarity between larger institutions and more informal networks is one of balance between power and agency. Public and corporate institutions naturally exercise power, given their scale and position within the interdependent networks of global society. But existing solidarity structures and systems enable concrete actions within the communities themselves, often out of reach of formal institutions. Not only the free culture movements need to help and enable each other, institutional powers also need to accept letting go of their trouble children, and enabling decentralized informal networks to intensify their social ties beyond specialization and a predetermined reading grid. Only then can we end infantilization and become adults as a species: by cooperating responsibly as members of a global society that embraces life, in all its complexity, uncertainty, and affectivity.

EPILOGUE

INTERNAL FREEDOM

hellekin

I am alive. I am grateful to be alive. I smile. I want to share this happiness. With anyone. I may lean on the left side of politics, and you may lean on the right side. It doesn't show on your face when I meet you in the street. We smile to each other. We exchange a salute. We start talking. During the course of the conversation, you hint to me of your political leaning. I frown. You hold your words. I'm sorry: the radical in me took over the human for a moment. I'd like to continue the conversation, why not? But I can't find my words. A second of silence and we're already out of sync. I have a doubt. Something in my past prevents me from connecting to you. Something in your past prevents you from connecting with me. We depart from each other. Both of us suffer a pinch of sadness.

I am alive. I am grateful to be alive. I smile. I want to share this happiness. With anyone. I may lean on the left side of the political spectrum, and you may lean on the right side. It doesn't show on your face when I meet you in the street. We smile to each other. We exchange a salute. We start talking. During the course of the conversation, you hint to me of your political leaning. I frown. You hold your words. "Oh," I shrug, "our paths may diverge on this topic, but I'm grateful we can share this moment together and learn from a different perspective." A second of silence, and you smile. "Let's walk together," you propose.

I smile back at you. Something in my past was triggered, I felt it in my heart. Something in your past let you leave the difference behind. As we let go, we enjoy our internal freedom.

A glance, a smile, a recognition: beyond the imposed

categories of society, we allow each other to not discriminate based on prejudice. Where is the matter that makes this possible? I want to call this matter: freedom.

LOVE LETTER TO COMPUTERS

Clément Renaud

An old WordPress installation turns into a zombie spam machine.

Interesting energy growing a beast of some sort.

Deleted accounts exist as active memories.

Transformative experience produces deceptive results.

Installed open-source software, took me three days: it never worked.

Technologies of intellect: learning to write, learning to write code, learning to write code and text.

Humans stuck in batches in traffic while information circulates around them.

Rivers, crabs and free fear on the PA. Inter-dependencies and versioning problems.

Aging commitments to unclear values.

Seeking something to recycle in the social data wasteland.

Pain-relievers and arnica for the back of your neck.

Vanishing values of approaching deadlines.

TOWARDS A POSSIBLE MANIFESTO; PROPOSING ARABFUTURISM(S) (CONVERSATION A)

Sulaiman Majali

"In hypernational ecstasy-"

"What about starting with where it's come from, something like that? -"

"-But they've called it a swarm, an influx-"

"There is something happening in Europe."

"We are distinctly distant from the mythologies of nationhood and home-"

"Stand up and step back."

"-What do we have"

"-The nation is dead, it is a citadel of illusion that has collapsed; pour me a drink and let us drink of its ruins. -"

"The nation is dead-"

"-Arabfuturism exponentially expands on discourse surrounding -"

"-Arabfuturism is accelerating the transformation of representation; beyond the logic of the state."

"-Surrounding the policing, observation and censoring of brown minds-"

"-...Indefinable in the emergence of an autonomous hybrid sedimentation of identities that is dismantling the boundaries and expanding the borderzones between constructs of culture and civilisation that have assembled a contrived European identity in opposition to an historic Other."

"Punctuation-,"

"Something about re-examining history?"

"-Arabfuturism is a re-examination and interrogation of narratives that surround oceans of historical fiction. It bulldozes cultural nostalgias that prop up a dubious political paralysis and works to solidify and progress a progressive force, towards being subjects and not objects of history"

"-History?"

"histories-"

"If the ultimate hegemonic power is the power to define and not the power to conquer; the map, the straight line, legitimacy and authenticity are questions that flutter between the virtualities and actualities of adopted identities."

"What are we proposing?"

"Arabfuturism is an impetus that seeks to accelerate the annihilation of the ideological apartheidic walls, whose delusional hallucinations make us cower in fear at the deafening loudness of our indifference; whilst we dance to the silence of our differences."

"A continuous motion"

"Accelerate-"

"-Accelerating-"

"- delusional hallucinations make us cower in fear at the deafening loudness of our indifference (whilst we dance to the silence of our differences.)"

"But there is something happening in Europe,-"

"Arabfuturism conceives instead, an origin in imagined space, towards the abyss of an imagined future"

"-Dancing on the ruins of the post-orientalist stage; in the desert of the unreal; high on the opulence of emptiness."

"- Violent births of countries; the expansions and contractions, the demise and deaths, -"

"-the demise and deaths of nations."

"The nation is dead-"

"-Something is happening in Europe-"

"-It is a citadel of illusion that has collapsed."

"-The internet as a public square,-"

"Arabfuturism celebrates the temporalities of our collaborative genealogies-"

"Mourning-"

"Present tense. Mourns the immortality of our insular mythologies of selfhood."

"-an emergent cultural aesthetic; accelerating the transformation of representation;-"

"-beyond the logic of the state."

THE COST OF FUTURE TENSE

hellekin

The freest person I've met perceived hosts on foreign networks in cryptic idioms like the forest of his childhood: each stone, each bird, each shadow had no secret for her.

The freest person on Earth knows three boundaries: the ocean and the breathing of its waves, and the roar of its depths; the stratosphere beyond which machines decay, out in the crushing silence of the solar wind; the skin, plastic and porous, the drum of desire dancing at the pulse of a broken heart.

The freest person I know doesn't look back to some flowing fiction of a continuous history, and ignores the prospect of a future past. She doesn't live to expectations: she stepped away from paved avenues to trace a tricky path, uncertain and bold. Lecturing an attentive group of customs officers on the futility of borders and the fate of money, the freest person passes through life in candid wonder.

There is debt to the children of men, wiping out fossil life, threatening theirs, even ours, for the convenience of an intense present with the blow of thunder. A choking smoke screen of comfort at the cost of future tense condemns our descent to oblivion with a cheering me-time. A blooming hell thrives as the gods laugh at our prophetic thin lines: technology would save us all, amen.

The freest person you've met always has time for you. Running here, standing there, bursting into laughter, frowning, crying along, sharing a quiet moment in the crank of an urban desert, his hello is always a relief. You could meet in the eyes of another solitude, another self; the presence of community in a smile, a word, a handshake would bring evidence of the Cosmos.

Sitting on a squeaky bed in solitude, with only the halo of an unseen moon to keep obscurity at bay, the freest person travels across space-time conserving memory of ancient temples in the confinement of her cell. Is the cost of freedom the burden of consciousness?

ANDROMEDA REPORT – GLIESE 832 C EXPEDITION

Yu Li

1. The return of the Convoy and the forgotten core

Dear Sir and Madam,

Here I am back from the journey where I sacrificed my heart and half-accomplished my mission as the Gliese 832 C expedition convoy.

I was to accompany them to find their next frontier where they could find the better system that could perfectly function for their society and the over-populated planet. But something made this mission unaccomplishable and I had to return, with dysfunctional parts of the body components infected, and having lost of part of the precious data that had needed to be protected.

2. The evolved species

Andromeda species have a core organ, a component used to store a high concentration of intelligence and the common knowledge of the species. It's a shared source that every individual can access to instantly exchange knowledge. Decision-making is also generated though this part of the organ while connected with external information and other useful resources. Since this part of the organ is able to absorb human emotion and information, during the period on Earth, these two parts are fused together, and can't be separated. And during the transition through Drake Passage wormhole, data transferring could not be accomplished, and the core was broken, meaning that some part of our Andromeda galaxy civilisation's knowledge has been also left behind in that ship.

3. Inspection of Planet Earth

To start the story, let me provide a small description of the situation of Planet Earth.

Planet Earth is a small-sized planet in the solar system located in the Milky Way Galaxy. This planet is 780 kiloparsecs away from our Andromeda Galaxy.

After several eras of industrialisation and over-exploitation of the planetary resource, the species on this planet, "humans", are facing a crucial moment in which they need to change the social system in order to survive and continue the expansion of the species.

The planet is facing over-exploitation of resources, and facing a fundamental shift away from the religious era that has influenced and disillusioned this species for thousands of years. This religious system is starting to reach a point where the system of faith and morality is challenged by the development of science and technology. This has resulted in wars and insoluble conflict occurring in different continents, and conflict between religious groups and these who are well advanced in scientific knowledge and value. The world is not the same as 2000 years ago when few scientific pioneers started observing the universe and were surrounded by a solid religious environment. In opposition, a small number of religious people are struggling to maintain their territory and their importance in the social scene, and this causes some regional crises and turmoil.

The society is facing a crossroads and a major decision to be made at individual, national and planetary level. It's an era in which the world is morphing from fog and innocence to an era of enlightenment through science and knowledge which will make it possible for the whole human civilisation to expand creatively and efficiently to a meaningful stage. What is needed is a way to ensure that science and technology are steadily integrated inside the society, and their beliefs are upgraded accordingly.

They are starting to have full consciousness of such a situation, and they are trying to find the way to achieve the ultimate freedom where sustainable civilisation development and planetary expansion can happen.

4. The contact of Gliese 832 C

At this crucial moment, however, a great scientific discovery shocked the whole world when a new planet was discovered, Gliese 832 C, home to a highly developed civilisation which has built its own sustainable energy supporting system (similar to a Dyson sphere), by harvesting energy from the stars to provide its growth.

The planetary space agency EPSA has announced that this new planetary system is 99.8% similar to the original Planet Earth. After this shocking news, all the industrial and federations are competing in a space race in order to have first contact with that planet.

5. Awaken spirit

Here I quote the Galactica survival law No. F42S , which was advised by Mr. Wolfgang Freeman Dyson in 3025.

This law says: Every intelligent species has to learn how to collaborate together with others as best they can, to achieve the level which is called Ulysse Entropy, a point where the synergy could bring this intelligent species to another level and rebuild the faith system, that could bring the whole species to another level of civilisation.

A secret meeting has been organised by several organisations and enterprises, such as the Planetary Disaster and

Monitoring centre, Extraterrestrial Defence Agency, Future-us (a planetary think tank that acts as an idea generation machine to provide counsel and advice for the different country governors), Planetary Lab (an institution that gathers all the scientists and engineers to do research on the next space frontier, including society study, anthropology, astrobiology, astrophysicists...etc. The research centre is based on the research network that CERN established in the 20th century, but the equipment has been largely modified and updated). In the middle of Himalaya mountains, after a long discussion with all the participants, they made the decision to pursue a secret mission.

6. Gliese 832 C Expedition

A secret intergalactic expeditionary mission comprised by a group of scientists, visionaries and engineers has been sent to Gliese 832 C, in order to make contact with the intelligent species there and learn from them a new way of organising human society and how to achieve sustainable resources and energy consumption.

The Gliese 832 C Expedition was sent from Planet Earth in 2035 by the Planetary Development Agency, a fusion of several pre-national space agencies from different countries with a common objective.

This mission was intended to fly to the Gliese 832 C, a newly discovered planet with an intelligent species with whom the PDA have successfully communicated. Gliese 832 is a planet where all activity is based on a distributed intelligence system in which every individual organises themselves and is fully conscious of what they are doing.

This planet offers an opportunity for the expedition members to learn how the populated society organises itself and collaborates to develop their society, and to bring this knowledge back to Planet Earth to help it find ways to sustain human society there.

I'm the civilisation intelligence convoy. I'm to accompany them for this mission, in order to ensure there are no dangerous happenings. This is my last mission, and I will return from their planet to solve the key problems that keep human civilisation stuck in this era.

My last mission includes encoding and backing up all the science and technology developed and involved in that civilisation's history, and transferring it to the next shell I will adapt in the future. I will pass through a tunnel and do the quantum leap to another civilisation, I will follow the Galactica map which is already embedded inside my system.

7. The Mysterious Romantic journey

During the mission, I fell in love with the Co-Captain. He convinced me to take hm with me to the Andromeda Galaxy. I agreed.

Our path towards Gliese 832 C was changed and redirected to the direction of Andromeda.

During our journey passing the border of Milky Way Galaxy, something happened on the ship. I'm disrupted by certain inexplicable events.

8. The virus

A discussion with my personal doctor tells me of shocking events: during the era in which I stayed on Earth with the shell of human, I was infected by several unknown human "viruses" which could cause the core dysfunction, threatening the loss of our own civilisation data.

160

Diagnostic results:

Since Human is an intelligent creature which is highly developed, this effect could transfer through biochemical contacts. That because part of my system is not fully functioning, some syndrome including the growing emotional capacity, which human called "love".

9. Disclosed hitchhiker

A few days later, during the transition in the wormhole while I'm uploading all the data, I discover that the co-captain has a suspicious background, suggesting that he is a representative of an ancient religious group that has been sent to destroy this ship and change its mission, a person who is technologically enhanced and able to transfer their own consciousness and mind to the intended target.

Underneath his gorgeous human shell, this shocking fact requires me to make a decision.

When I dig further into the situation, it becomes worse, I find the other seven pilots have also been infected by him, most of them are in a critical state. I need to make a decision...

10. Decision making

But time is too late, I have to leave, the quantum leap consumes a lot of energy. The only way is to destroy the infected co-captains, but without these captains, the ship won't able to go its final destination. The only solution is to freeze the whole ship and all the crew, and then go back to the ship one day and bring them back. I decide to sacrifice my heart and part of the organ which has been infected by the virus. I kill the Co-Captain and keep the hundreds of crew on board... frozen, and don't know when there will be a chance to awaken them again.

I am ready to do the quantum leap, and the ship is frozen in the wormhole...

11. The speech

Here I am, I successfully leapt to Andromeda! I'm alive. Now, I have to report the event and I will apply to go back to that wormhole to release my ship's crew and continue this journey.

I want your full support and the right to command a 1000 ship convoy in order to pass through that Drake Passage and bring them back.

...

APPENDIX

CALL FOR PARTICIPATION

Call for mini-essays on "the cost of freedom" in free knowledge movements in honor of Bassel Khartabil, October 2015

Dear friends,

I'm helping organize a book titled "The Cost of Freedom" in honor of Bassel Khartabil, a contributor to numerous free/open knowledge projects worldwide and in Syria, where he's been a political prisoner since 2012, missing and in grave danger since October 3. You can read about Bassel at `https://www.eff.org/offline/bassel-khartabil`, `https://blog.wikimedia.org/2015/10/08/bassel-missing-syria/`, `https://www.amnesty.org/en/documents/MDE24/2603/2015/en/`, and lots more at `https://en.wikipedia.org/wiki/Bassel_Khartabil` and `http://freebassel.org/`

Much of the book is going to be created at a face-to-face Book Sprint in Marseille Nov 2-6; some info about that and the theme/title generally at `http://costoffreedom.cc/`

We're also asking people like yourself who have been fighting in the trenches of various free knowledge movements (culture, software, science, etc.) to contribute brief essays for inclusion in the book. One form an essay might take is a paragraph on each of:

- An issue you've faced that was challenging to you in your free knowledge work, through the lens on "cost"; perhaps a career or time opportunity cost, or the cost of dealing with unwelcoming or worse participants, or the cost of "peeling off layer upon layer the proprietary way of life" as put in `http://www.adamhyde.net/open-is-not-a-license/`
- How you addressed this challenge, or perhaps have yet

to do so completely

- Advice to someone starting out in free knowledge; perhaps along the lines of had you understood the costs, what would you have done differently

But feel free to be maximally creative within the theme. We don't have a minimum or a maximum required length for contributed essays, but especially do not be shy about concision or form. If all we get is haiku that might be a problem, or there might be a message in that of some sort.

Other details: The book will be PUBLISHED on Nov 6. We need your contribution no later than **Nov 5 at 11:00 UTC** (Paris: noon; New York: 6AM; Tokyo: 9PM) to be included. The book will be released under CC0; giving up the "right" to sue anyone for any use whatsoever of your contribution is a cost of entry...or one of those proprietary layers to be peeled back. Send contributions to book@costoffreedom.cc

Feel free to share this with other people who you know have something to say on this topic. We're especially looking for voices underrepresented in free knowledge movements.

Cheers,

Mike

p.s. Please spread the word about #freebassel even if you can't contribute to the book!

source: `http://gondwanaland.com/mlog/2015/10/29/cost-of-freedom/`

CREATIVE COMMONS CC0

This book is released under the terms of the CC0 License, and therefore dedicated to the Public Domain.

www.ingramcontent.com/pod-product-compliance
Lightning Source LLC
Chambersburg PA
CBHW032012170526
45157CB00002B/665